The Observers Series
TROPICAL FISHES

About the Book

There can be no doubt about the visual appeal of a well-stocked tropical fish tank, and this practical book provides an introduction to the beginner with little knowledge of the hobby. It is also a book of reference for the experienced aquarist. As well as describing how an attractive tropical aquarium can be set up, stocked and maintained, 90 popular species of fish are illustrated in full colour and described in detail. Information is given on the care of each species, feeding, the conditions likely to induce spawning, and how to rear the young and bring them to maturity. All the species included in this book have proved their worth over the years, and it would be possible to have a lifetime's enjoyment of the hobby without keeping any tropical fish species that is not described in this handy little reference book.

About the Author

The late Neil Wainwright was a lifelong tropical fish enthusiast and was fortunate enough to spend many years abroad where he was able to study these fascinating and colourful species in their natural habitat. This latest edition has been revised and updated by Dr Gwynne Vevers, until his recent retirement Assistant Director of Science and Curator of the Aquarium at London Zoo.

D1393966

The *Observer's* series was launched in 1937 with the publication of *The Observer's Book of Birds*. Today, fifty years later, paperback *Observers* continue to offer practical, useful information on a wide range of subjects, and with every book regularly revised by experts, the facts are right up-to-date. Students, amateur enthusiasts and professional organisations alike will find the latest *Observers* invaluable.

'Thick and glossy, briskly informative' – *The Guardian*

'If you are a serious spotter of any of the things the series deals with, the books must be indispensable' – *The Times Educational Supplement*

O B S E R V E R S

TROPICAL FISHES

Neil Wainwright

With 90 colour illustrations by Baz East

BLOOMSBURY BOOKS
LONDON

PENGUIN BOOKS

Published by the Penguin Group
Penguin Books Ltd, 27 Wrights Lane, London W8 5TZ, England
Penguin Books USA Inc., 375 Hudson Street, New York, New York 10014, USA
Penguin Books Australia Ltd, Ringwood, Victoria, Australia
Penguin Books Canada Ltd, 2801 John Street, Markham, Ontario, Canada L3R 1B4
Penguin Books (NZ) Ltd, 182–190 Wairau Road, Auckland 10, New Zealand

Penguin Books Ltd, Registered Offices: Harmondsworth, Middlesex, England

First published as *The Observer's Book of Tropical Fishes* 1976
Reprinted 1978, 1983 (revised format)
Reprinted with revisions 1987

This edition published by Bloomsbury Books, an imprint of
Godfrey Cave Associates, 42 Bloomsbury Street, London, WC1B 3QJ,
under licence from Penguin Books Limited, 1992

1 3 5 7 9 10 8 6 4 2

Printed and bound in Great Britain by
BPCC Hazells Ltd
Member of BPCC Ltd

ISBN 1-8547-1078-8

Contents

Preface

The keeping of tropical fishes is a hobby that is increasing in popularity and its devotees range from schoolchildren to nonagenarians. This practical book has been written as an introduction to aquariums for the layman whose knowledge of the hobby is limited, and as a book of reference for the aquarist with some experience of the subject.

The vital requirements for maintaining fish life under the best possible conditions are described in sufficient detail to enable a tropical freshwater tank to be installed satisfactorily and without undue expense. The temperature of the water required for certain types of fish is given, and the types of plants best suited to them.

The fish described here are the long established favourites of the aquarium. All have proved their worth over the years, and it would be possible to have a lifetime's enjoyment of the hobby without considering any fish species that is not mentioned in this book. Some of these fish can live happily in a community tank, while others needing specialist care must be segregated, and are not always suitable for the beginner to rear.

Sufficient information is given about each species to enable the fish to be cared for adequately, and the conditions likely to induce spawning are also described. Particular mention is made of suitable diets necessary for rearing the young and bringing them to maturity.

Periodically a certain species of fish will come into

'fashion' and aquarists will clamour to obtain specimens of it, often paying inflated prices for the privilege. After a few seasons it may be found that, for a variety of reasons, it is far from being an ideal fish for the average fishkeeper, and the species sinks back into relative obscurity.

It is hoped that this book will serve as a valuable guide to fish-keeping for a considerable number of newcomers to the hobby, and that they will gain much pleasure and knowledge from watching and caring for these attractive tropical freshwater fishes.

Introduction

Freshwater aquarium fishes may be defined as those species whose natural habitat is in freshwater rivers or lakes, yet they may be kept satisfactorily in the somewhat artificial conditions of an aquarium. Many of the species originated in warm tropical or sub-tropical regions, and these fishes need more care and attention than do coldwater types such as the goldfish or tench, which may also be kept in an aquarium. As a very broad rule it may be said that the tropical freshwater species are more colourful than the coldwater types, and are of smaller size, permitting a greater number and variety of fishes to be kept in an aquarium of average size.

It is important to realize that although a fish species originated in a particular area, the specimens seen in an aquarium almost certainly do not come from that area, and usually bear little resemblance to the original form of the fish. It is extremely unlikely that any swordtail purchased in a water-life shop was actually imported from Mexico, for most tropical freshwater fish can be bred in captivity; only when breeding of a particular species has been found extremely difficult or impossible is it necessary to import wild stock. Selective breeding over the years also means that as regards the size and shape of the fins, colouring, and other external factors, aquarium species may differ widely from their wild ancestors.

All aquarium species have a popular name such as neon tetra or black widow, and some may have more than one such name in fairly common use. While

9

valuable for day to day use, these common names are not practical for the accurate identification of the fish, and such titles as tetra, barb, glassfish, etc., can often be misleading.

For more accurate identification the binominal nomenclature of Carl von Linné has been used since 1758. This system divides animals and plants into groups in such a way that their relationship can be readily established.

Tropical freshwater fishes belong to the large group of bony fishes called the Teleostei, and this in turn is divided into a number of orders and sub-orders. The sub-orders are divided into families, which are further broken down into genera (in the singular, a genus) and species. Members of a given order share certain characteristics which become more apparent in the family and even more so in the genera.

Scientific nomenclature is not perfect and sometimes causes some confusion, for as progress is made with ichthyological research it sometimes becomes necessary to re-classify certain fish. Such name changes are not always universally accepted or quickly adopted, and consequently scientific synonyms are reasonably common, which may lead the uninitiated to believe, for example, that *Chanda lala* and *Ambassis lala* are different species, whereas these titles are scientific synonyms. The system does, however, provide the best available method of classifying and identifying fish.

Scientific names consist of two words (e.g. *Colisa lalia*), the first indicating the genus and the second the species. There may be several species within a genus so that there is also a *Colisa labiosa* and a *Colisa fasciata*. If a fish is known to belong to a particular genus, but its species cannot be accurately identified or has not been given a name, the fish would be described by its generic name followed by the word species.

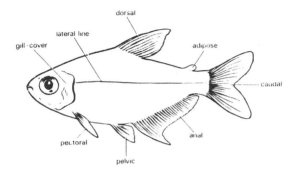

External Characteristics of the Fish

Nearly all fish have seven fins, four of which are paired. A fin consists of a number of rays, connected by membrane, and in some species a number of the rays are much harder than the normal and are described as spines. Identification of a species is sometimes based on the number of rays and spines in the various fins.

The most prominent fin is normally the tail or caudal fin. Along the middle line of the body is the anal fin, which is set forward of the tail, while on the top of the body is the dorsal fin which is occasionally in two parts. These are all single fins. The paired fins, which are situated one on each side of the body, are the pectorals, placed just behind the head, and the pelvic or ventral fins on the belly of the fish.

A few species have an extra fin, the adipose, set between the dorsal and caudal fins; the adipose fin has no rays or spines.

Not always clearly visible is the lateral line, a row of perforated scales running the length of the body on each side. This forms a sensitive organ that permits the fish to detect vibrations in the water or changes of pressure. With some species there may be marked colour differences above and below the lateral line.

The other prominent external features are the gill-covers. Water is taken in through the mouth and passes over the gills where the oxygen is extracted, carbon dioxide then being released into the water by way of the gill openings at the back of the head.

The Aquarium Tank

If fish are to be kept in comfortable and healthy surroundings some consideration must be given to the tank, its lighting and heating equipment, and the water in which the fish will live.

Tanks are available in a wide range of sizes and shapes, and the type selected is largely a matter of individual preference. All-glass tanks are excellent, but angle-framed aquaria are very satisfactory as long as the metal-work has not been treated with a toxic paint. The tank must be free of leaks and, before being taken into use, it should be sterilized with warm water tinged slightly pink with permanganate of potash crystals.

A hood or tank cover is essential, for this helps to prevent excessive evaporation, restrains active species that may occasionally try to leap out of the tank, and provides the housing for the form of lighting to be used. Lighting of the tank not only adds to its appearance but also encourages plant and fish growth.

Tropical fish need heated water, usually at a temperature of between 21°C (69°F) and 23°C (73°F). A combined heater and thermostat is used to maintain the temperature and this should be of the type that allows adjustment of the figure at which the thermostat is brought into action.

A very few fish species prefer an extremely weak saline water, this being obtained by putting a slightly heaped teaspoonful of kitchen salt to every five litres of water in the tank, but the great majority are perfectly at home in ordinary tap water. It is advisable to draw off the quantity required from the tap and store it in buckets, covered with a piece of muslin to exclude dust, until such time as the smell of chlorine characteristic of town supplies has evaporated. If the local water is exceptionally hard, a more suitable water for fish is obtained by mixing together equal quantities of tap water and distilled water.

A tank must be set up by easy stages. The base of the sterilized tank is covered with a layer of well-washed aquarium gravel. This last should be sloped gently from back to front of the tank and for realism should be left with an irregular surface rather than a smooth one. Before filling the tank with water, lay a sheet of stout brown paper on the bottom so that the gravel is not disturbed.

A cup or tumbler is placed in the centre of the sheet of paper and cold, de-chlorinated water is poured gently into this until it overflows the edges and starts to fill the tank. After a short while the cup or tumbler can be removed, then the filling resumed until the upper surface of the tank water is level with the under edge of the top horizontal metal angle framing bar of the tank. The paper can then be lifted free of the water, and will bring with it a certain amount of dust and other rubbish. The heater and pre-set thermostat are laid in place on the gravel (but not buried in it) and the heater is switched on. If the tank is filled in this way, there will be a minimum of disturbance to the gravel.

Some fish-keepers embellish the tank with so-called ornaments or natural rockwork. The number, type and method of arrangement of these items is largely a matter of personal choice, though most fish appreciate a number of places in which they can hide, and these can easily be incorporated into the layout. What is important is that all such items should be thoroughly sterilized with hot water before being put in place.

Once the tank has been allowed to settle down for a few days, some aquatic plants can be introduced. These plants serve a dual purpose. They absorb the carbon dioxide exhaled by the fish and in return give up additional oxygen to the water. The plant roots are nourished by the fish excreta and the growing plants not only serve a decorative purpose, but help to conceal the unsightly heater cables.

Several varieties of aquatic plant can be purchased from water-life shops, two of the most popular being *Vallisneria* and *Myriophyllum*. The plants should be set out in clumps towards the back of the tank. For each plant a small hole is raked in the gravel, the plant roots are spread well out and the gravel is firmed back over them. A small lead collar at the base of each plant will help to anchor it in place.

With the tank filled, and the plants set-out in the gravel, the fish can be introduced once the water has reached the desired temperature. The fish will almost certainly be bought from the retailer in a plastic bag. This last should be floated in the tank for about ten minutes, then it is opened (with the mouth of the bag under water) so that the fish can swim quietly out into their new home.

Fish-keepers recognize two types of tank, the community tank housing representatives of different species that are known to live together harmoniously, and the specialist tank in which all the fish are of the same species.

Oxygen

Oxygen is essential for fish life and, as pointed out above, the fish extract this from the water. If a high percentage of the oxygen in the water is exhausted, the fish will die.

If the number of fish kept in the tank is not too great this cannot happen because fresh oxygen is absorbed from the atmosphere at the surface of the water. The greater the water surface the more oxygen that is absorbed, and in consequence the more fish life that can be satisfactorily maintained. The depth of water in a fish tank is unimportant provided that there is sufficient room for the fish to move around comfortably.

Fish suffering from lack of oxygen tend to gulp at the surface of the water. All fish will do this on occasion, but if this practice is widespread it must be regarded as a warning sign that cannot be ignored. The most likely cause of lack of oxygen is that the water has become polluted with rotting food, etc., causing the oxygen to be depleted or replaced with noxious gases. Alternatively, too many fish are being kept in the tank for its size.

Although aquatic plants feed additional oxygen into the water, their contribution is relatively small. Many aquarists make use of aerating equipment to boost up the available oxygen supplies, but in a properly maintained tank such equipment is by no means essential. Like all mechanical equipment, aerators can break down and the fish may suffer some distress if too much reliance has been placed on aeration by such methods.

Diet

An adequate and varied diet is necessary to keep fish healthy, but over-feeding is a frequent source of trouble. Two meals per day is normal, but the fish should never be given more food at any time than they can consume in five minutes.

Foods are of two types, dried and live.

Dried foods are prepared to a number of differing formulae and may be in powder or flake form. Some of the cheapest foods have a high percentage of biscuit meal in their make-up and these have little nutritional value. Other foods show a preponderance of animal or vegetable matter, and it will be found that certain species of fish show a marked preference for one or other of these foods.

Other dried foods are in tablet form and are often

described as freeze-dried diets. A tablet of this type is pressed against the glass on the inside of the tank and will be gradually nibbled away by the fish.

Some fish species can thrive on an exclusive diet of dry food, but such species should be given an occasional live meal to keep them in perfect health. Other fish species live exclusively on live food. When conditioning prospective parents for breeding purposes, the percentage of live food in the diet is increased sharply.

Live foods include such items as brine shrimps, daphnia, micro-worm, tubifex worms, rotifers, cyclops and infusoria (tiny aquatic animals). Chopped earthworm is also favoured by many species. Live foods may be purchased or reared by the aquarist, but in all cases it is necessary that the food be of a size suitable for the gullets of the fish to which it is to be fed.

Breeding

Most aquarists become interested in the problems of breeding their fish. Initially, such interest will be directed towards increasing the number of fish owned, but later a more scientific approach may be adopted so that the fish are bred with the intention of improving certain desirable characteristics. This latter form of breeding is usually described as *controlled breeding* and involves some study of genetics. *Uncontrolled breeding* infers a casual mating that produces young that may, or may not, have the best characteristics of their parents.

As regards the production of young fish, species fall into two main classes.

The smaller class comprises the *viviparous* or *livebearer* species. With these the female produces the young as fully formed, free-swimming fish. The fry are extremely active and able to take certain foods from birth. Such births are commonplace in a community tank, given a sexually mature male and female of a viviparous species.

Newly hatched fry immediately dart towards the nearest shelter, usually among the plants. Adult fish often show strong cannibalistic tendencies, and the parents themselves often have no compunction in eating their offspring. Many of the fry will fall victim to the adults, but some may survive to reach a size where they no longer suggest a tasty tit-bit for the larger fish.

Most species are *oviparous* or *egg-laying*. With these the female deposits the eggs, which are then fertilized by the male. The fry eventually hatch out, but for a time they are unable to swim or to take food and exist by absorbing the contents of their egg-sacs. Once free swimming, the fry need ordinary diets so that they grow on to maturity. The chances of eggs or newly hatched fry surviving in a community tank are negligible.

The fry, both of live-bearer and egg-laying species, need to be fed on suitable diets and perhaps the best of these are the tubed foods sold specially for that purpose.

Mating is nearly always preceded by a courtship ritual involving the display of fins, the circling of each other, and so on, but usually culminates in the female being driven through the plants at considerable speed, during which time the eggs are laid and fertilized.

With some species courtship can be a very rough process, and a reluctant female can be so savagely mauled that she will die of her injuries.

According to species, the requirements for successful breeding vary slightly, but a general outline of the techniques to be adopted may be given here.

The first requirement is a breeding tank, with its separate heater. The tank may be quite small, the base should be covered with a layer of coarse gravel, no rockwork or aquarium ornaments should be installed, but aquatic plants must be provided when oviparous species are to be bred.

For the live-bearers, planting of the tank is usually unnecessary, but a breeding trap must be installed. In one form of this two inclined plates are set towards the bottom of the trap, with a small gap between their inside edges so that as the fish are born they can escape into the lower part of the tank, where the adult fish cannot get at them. Another form of trap consists of a number of plastic rods set side by side with narrow gaps between their edges. Breeding traps are normally made of clear plastic.

It is customary to raise the temperature of the breeding tank to a figure slightly above that of the tank from which the parents are taken. To encourage spawning among the egg-laying species, a glass divider is placed midway across the tank so that male and female are kept in separate compartments.

The parents to be are kept well fed on a diet that is richer than usual in live food. Live-bearer species usually need little encouragement to breed, but the egg-layers may need segregation for a number of days. When it is apparent that the fish are becoming interested in each other the glass partition can be removed, this being done overnight.

Spawning by the *egg-laying species* usually takes place in the early hours of the morning. With some species the parent fish must be netted and returned to their main tank immediately spawning is finished, but with others the adults should be left with the eggs. Such factors as these are considered in the notes on the fish species of which the greater part of this book is comprised.

The number of eggs laid, and their size, depend on the species involved. It is a common practice to remove the eggs from the breeding tank to an incubating tank of the same water temperature so that the eggs are left undisturbed for hatching.

Most fish eggs are adhesive or semi-adhesive, and will stick to the plants or sides of the glass tank. It is sometimes possible to move the plants carrying the eggs without undue trouble, but to make the job easier nylon mats or mops are commonly used. A nylon mop, as its name suggests, is simply a small mop-head; two or more of these put into the breeding tank will collect and trap many of the eggs. A nylon mat is put at the bottom of the tank for those species that deposit non-adhesive eggs, as the latter merely fall to the bottom of the tank and can be collected on the mat, which is transferred to the incubating tank.

Live-bearers are less of a problem than the *egg-layers*. The impregnated female will develop a prominent dark spot (the gravid spot) on the belly, and with this indication of a successful mating the male fish can be transferred to the main tank, leaving the female undisturbed to give birth to her young.

The care of the fry will vary according to the species. In some cases a depression will be made in the aquarium gravel and the eggs transferred to this by the male, who will make himself responsible for the eggs until they have hatched. He may even attack the female if she approaches the eggs. Other species blow a nest of bubbles at the surface of the water and transfer the eggs to this. Again, this is usually the responsibility of the male, though with some species both parents share the duty. Another interesting example of parental care is evidenced by the *mouth-brooders*. When alarmed, the fry of such species will swim into their mother's mouth and she will keep them there until the apparent danger has passed. Such exceptions apart, it is true to say that the average fish species show little interest in, or care for, their young.

For successful breeding the special requirements of the particular species need to be considered, and any departure from a tried technique rarely proves successful. The notes on the individual species will be found helpful.

Maintenance of an Aquarium

The word maintenance is usually taken to mean those routine operations that ensure the well-being of the fish. It includes the periodical and proper cleaning of the tank, the prevention of water pollution, the thinning out, as necessary, of the aquatic plants, and so on. Routine maintenance takes up very little time each day, but it is essential.

Fish Ailments

Fish are liable to suffer from a wide range of ailments, many of which are preventable. A number of minor ailments are simple to treat and the problem is one of diagnosis rather than of medication. The subject is too large to cover in a book of this type, and the writer's *Tropical Aquariums* (also published by Frederick Warne, but now out-of-print) covers this and other aspects of fish-keeping, at greater length.

One point is, however, worth noting. Any fish showing signs of sickness should be removed immediately to a quarantine tank, this simply being a small heated tank in which the fish can be kept in isolation. Sickness is usually indicated by general listlessness, drooping of the fins, and dull glazed eyes. Once the fish has been cured of its illness and has been returned to the main tank, the quarantine tank must be thoroughly sterilized before it is used again.

It is also a sound idea to make use of a quarantine tank when new fish are acquired, whatever the source from which they may have been obtained. A few days in the quarantine tank will show if the fish are in perfect health, and only when the owner is satisfied on this point should the newcomers be introduced into the main tank. Failure to take this precaution could mean that diseased fish could be put in with the healthy stock, and the mortality rate amongst the latter could be high.

American Flag Fish

American Flag Fish

Jordanella floridae   CYPRINODONTIDAE
Other name: Flag fish
Original distribution: Florida

This fish is probably best kept in a specialist tank,
being rather aggressive, but a pair will settle down
reasonably well in a community tank as long as the
other inhabitants are of approximately the same size.
For a sub-tropical species the flag fish prefers a low
temperature, from 20°C to 22°C. Vegetable matter is
an essential part of the diet and the fish thrives in a
tank rich in algae; it will also eat live food.

The species belongs to a toothed family and has a
short, rounded snout, a large fan-shaped caudal fin,
and grows to a maximum size of 6.35 cm. Seen by
reflected light, the body is blue to yellowish-green
with an iridescent sheen. The male has a green
luminous dot on a brownish base on each scale, with
the borders of the scales partly edged with red. As
they are arranged in regular longitudinal rows the
markings are very distinctive. The anal, caudal and

dorsal fins are marked with dotted red bands. The colouring is intensified when the fish is in breeding condition.

The female of the species is paler in colour than the male and has irregular markings of a dark colour that give a marbled effect. She also has a small dark spot on the dorsal fin.

Spawning will be encouraged by the segregation of the sexes for some days, and conditioning the brood fish by giving them live food only. Breeding should take place in a thickly planted tank. The eggs may sometimes be laid on the plants, but normally the male will fan a depression in the gravel with his tail, and the female will deposit her eggs in this 'nest'. She must be removed immediately after spawning. The male guards the eggs until they hatch out and is a good parent in that he will neither eat the eggs nor attack the fry. The young fish can be reared successfully on algae and freshly hatched brine shrimps.

Angel Fish

Pterophyllum scalare   CICHLIDAE
Original distribution: Amazon

A timid, delicate fish, but a stately, slow-swimming species that makes it one of the most attractive of all aquarium fish. Several fancy varieties (such as 'black', 'lace', 'marbled' and 'veil-tail' angels) are bred. While young they are excellent community fish, but they can grow to 15 cm in length and would need

Angel Fish

transferring to a special tank long before reaching
that size. Angel fish are tolerant of a wide temperature
range but need a varied diet. The characteristic dark
bars of the fish almost disappear when the fish is
frightened.

Sexing these fish is extremely difficult and the following description can be taken as applicable to both sexes. The thin body is disc-like in shape and the fins long and flowing backwards in graceful curves. The body is silvery with numerous bluish flecks on the side and is striped with evenly spaced black bars, the first of which passes through the red-rimmed eye with the last one on the caudal fin.

The veil-tail angel has considerably elongated fins and is usually of a marbled colour. With the black angel the characteristic bars can barely be seen, the fish being of a deep velvety black, while in the lace angel the fins show a black lace pattern with the body colouring darker than that of the ordinary angel fish.

To select a pair for breeding it is necessary to allow the fish to pair off by mutual attraction. Pairs who mate tend to stay together for life and are usually good parents. Courtship play is often boisterous.

Dim lighting is necessary for the breeding tank which must be densely planted with broad-leaved plants. The adhesive eggs will hatch out in some 48 hours and the parents may be seen to gather the fry in their mouths and transfer them to other plants. If the parents are frightened in any way they may eat both eggs and fry, but otherwise they are excellent guardians. The fry are voracious feeders and after being fed on infusoria for a short time they should be given plenty of brine shrimps and micro-worm.

Argentine Pearl

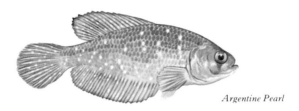

Argentine Pearl

Cynolebias bellotti　　　　　　　Cyprinodontidae
Original distribution: South America

The Argentine pearl is a peaceful fish but one that is not suitable for a community tank unless it is in a small shoal of its own kind. When shoals are large there may be some tendency to quarrelling. The male and female are so dissimilar in colour, etc., that they can easily be mistaken for different species. Argentine pearls prefer a diet consisting mainly of live food and a water temperature of between 21°C and 26°C.

The adult male grows to a body length of 7.5 cm. The general body colour is a deep shade of green, darker on the back, with smallish light blue or pearly white spots scattered over the body and vertical fins. There is a dark edging to the caudal and anal fins. A dark stripe passes through the eye. When in breeding condition, the colour changes to a dark blue.

The female fish has a dark stripe across the eye. She is smaller than the male. The colour is a yellowish-green with irregular marking of dark brown vertical stripes; the underside of the mouth is of a slate blue colour.

This is not an easy fish to breed in an aquarium tank and even if the eggs hatch, the fry may not reach maturity. This is because of the unusual breeding habits of the fish in its natural habitat.

The breeding tank should be filled with slightly saline water at a temperature of 22°C; a deep sandy bottom must be provided. Spawning may take place over several days, the eggs being laid singly. Once spawning has finished, the adults must be removed and the tank drained gradually over a period of ten days. The sand is left moist and after a few days the tank is gradually refilled with clean rain water. This refilling is done over a three-day period. When the eggs hatch the fry should be fed with brine shrimp and daphnia.

Badis

Badis

Badis badis   NANDIDAE
Original distribution: India

This is a hardy little fish, peaceful with others but sometimes quarrelsome with its own kind, though the battles that ensue are more mock than serious and little damage is ever done. It prefers a densely planted tank having plenty of hiding-places, with a water temperature of between 20°C and 26°C. The fish are voracious feeders but will usually take only live food, more especially when they are in a breeding condition. This species is apt to change colour, not only when breeding, but also according to its surroundings. It is at its best when kept in a small shoal.

Badis can be so variable in colour that it is difficult to describe the norm. Reddish to almost mauve represents the range, and in some cases the markings may take the form of red spots on a darker base. The dorsal fin may also carry bluish-green bands, while a dark band of colour passes through the eye. Each scale carries a dark edging. The head and mouth openings are small, the back is slightly arched, and the underparts of the male are drawn in slightly. The long dorsal fin is an attractive feature.

During breeding the male shows a considerable colour change, while the female retains her normal colouring which is simpler than that of the male. She is also recognizable by her fuller belly. During courtship the female may be badly mauled if she is not larger than the male.

Technically the Badis can be described as a cave-dweller, and it is essential to provide an artificial cave. The breeding tank, which should have a temperature of 29°C, must be densely planted and a large flowerpot, placed on its side, provides a suitable spawning place. The fish will spawn upside down on the inside of the pot. The female must be removed immediately after spawning, but the male should be left until the eggs have hatched. It is essential to feed the fry on infusoria as they are unable to take anything larger.

Beacon Fish

Hemigrammus ocellifer   CHARACIDAE
Other name: Head and tail light fish
Original distribution: Guyana, Amazon Basin

Beacon Fish

The fish takes its alternative name from the manner in which the bright orange of the eye and tail spot is reflected. It is a popular community fish and is both peaceful and hardy. It thrives best in a water temperature of between 20°C and 26°C, and a sudden drop in temperature is likely to cause the fish considerable distress. While it will take all normal fish diets, a high percentage of live food should be included in its meals. Beacon fish are among the longest lived of the family.

The male fish is recognizable by a slightly more pointed dorsal fin and a faint spot on the anal fin. Another difference between the male and female is that the former is both slimmer and smaller than the female.

30

A golden yellow spot is situated near the caudal peduncle, while the upper edge of the gill-covers may also show a similar spot. The iris of the eye is yellow and red, while the body colouring is a light greenish-brown; there is also an indistinct brown line that runs the length of the body. With some specimens the basic body colouring may tend to be rather silvery.

This species is comparatively easy to breed but it is advisable to use two males to every female. The water temperature of the breeding tank should be about 25°C. The breeding tank needs to be rather larger than usual, with a water depth of 25 cm. Fine-leaved plants are required, rooted towards one end of the tank to provide anchorage for the adhesive eggs. The adult fish should be removed after spawning. Eggs hatch out in about three days. Rearing of the fry is not difficult, but they should be moved on to adult food by very gradual stages.

Black Widow

Gymnocorymbus ternetzi   CHARACIDAE
Original distribution: Paraguay

A well-established favourite in the aquarium tank, the black widow is small, hardy and peaceful, and is very suitable for a community tank. It will eat any type of food but thrives best on live foods. The fish is rather sensitive to foul water conditions and when affected in this way it will tend to swim head downwards. Specimens up to 3 cm long show the colouring at its best; however, the fish can grow up to

Black Widow

6.5 cm long and the larger ones develop a humped body and the colour fades to grey. The original stock has been improved by the development of species with superb fins.

The body colour is silvery-green with a beautiful sheen, and there are black bands across the body. The fish has bright, red-rimmed eyes. In the smaller specimens the back of the body, the dorsal, hooked anal and adipose fins are jet black, though all these markings will fade with age. The caudal fin is transparent and sometimes difficult to see.

Sexing is not easy, and size and coloration are not necessarily good guides. The reliable method is to determine the females by the swelling of the belly when it is filled with spawn.

The breeding tank should have a water temperature of about 24°C and should be densely planted towards one end; it is also advisable to have some floating plants. The eggs are semi-adhesive and while some will attach themselves to the plants, others will fall to the bottom. The parents scatter the eggs freely, about ten at a time. Both brood fish should be removed once spawning is finished. The eggs will normally hatch in two to three days. The fry are not difficult to rear but should be started on infusoria before graduating to sifted daphnia and micro-worms.

Bloodfin

Aphyocharax rubripinnis   CHARACIDAE
Original distribution: Argentina

Bloodfin

This is a lively but peaceful fish and is ideally suited for the community tank as it rarely grows to a size greater than 5.5 cm. It prefers a well-lighted tank and is at its most natural state when in a small shoal of its own kind. A water temperature of 25°C suits it admirably. It is not fussy as regards food.

The fish takes its popular name from the colour of the fins, for with the exception of the pectorals these are blood red in colour. The fins also serve as a guide to distinguishing between the sexes, for in the female the colour is less deep, while the male almost invariably has a white tip to the anal and ventral fins.

This is a slim-bodied fish of silvery-green colour

with a metallic gleam. The head is well rounded and the mouth rather small.

The breeding habits are interesting. Two males are used to one female and a fairly large tank is filled to a depth of 15 cm, and is deeply planted with both tall and short growing varieties. The water temperature should be maintained at 24°C.

Spawning normally takes place in the early hours of the morning. The fish leap clear of the water and come together above the surface. As they fall back into the tank the female scatters a considerable number of non-adhesive transparent eggs; these eggs will be spread over a wide area. The adults must be removed as soon as spawning is finished.

The fry will hatch in about three days and will remain close to the water surface. Their first food should consist of infusoria, and this should be followed by micro-worm and very finely sieved dry food. The baby fish grow quickly and come to sexual maturity at a very early age.

It is more difficult to persuade the fish to breed than to raise the resulting fry.

Brown Acara

Aequidens portalegrensis CICHLIDAE
Other names: *Acara portalegrensis,* Port, Black or
    Green Acara
Original distribution: South-eastern Brazil

This is not a good community species, chiefly on account of its size, for it can grow from 13 cm to

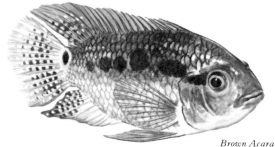

Brown Acara

15.5 cm. Although it is large, it is a timid fish and when first placed in the tank it may try to hide itself away for some days. It is the most peaceful member of the genus *Aequidens* which includes the blue acara, *Aequidens pulcher*. This fish differs only in colour, and is more truly green than blue.

Although called the 'brown' acara, the adjective is not altogether a good one for immature fish of the species are a uniform shade of dark olive green.

Sexing is not easy, though the anal fin of the female is shorter and more rounded than that of the male, and the fin colouring is less bright. The scales are comparatively large, while the fins are greenish and marbled with various colours. From the eye to the caudal peduncle is a wide stripe below which are vertical bars of dark colour. At the caudal peduncle there is a dark patch surrounded by dots of yellow or green. The background colour of the mature fish is reddish-brown.

One really unusual feature of this species is that once a pair has spawned they usually stay as a mating couple until death.

Breeding couples should be fed heavily on live foods. Courtship and mating can be violent, and rockwork or other items liable to damage the fish must be removed from the breeding tank. It is advisable to ensure that the brood fish are of approximately the same size. Plants need not be used in the breeding tank, but a piece of flat slate on which the eggs can be laid is put in the tank. The adhesive eggs are fanned by the parents and when hatched the fry are moved daily by their parents.

The brood fish should be removed from the breeding tank when the fry are free swimming, and the young fish can be brought on to maturity with infusoria, screened daphnids and micro-worms.

Bumble Bee

Bumble Bee

Brachygobius nunus   GOBIIDAE
Original distribution: Malaysia

Other species of *Brachygobius* are to be found in aquarium tanks, but they are so similar in appearance and characteristics that there is no point in trying to differentiate between them as they are all termed 'bumble bees'.

This cannot be described as a good community fish and it is certainly not an active one. The pelvic fins form a kind of suction disc and the bumble bee will remain motionless on a rock or plant for an hour or more at a time. It may become reasonably active when feeding.

A teaspoonful of salt in the tank will be appreciated by the fish, and it also likes plenty of hiding-places. A maximum size of 4.5 cm is attained. A high percentage of animal matter is required in the diet.

The body colour is a golden yellow and it carries four bands that are normally deep black; these bands are of irregular width and in poor specimens their outline may be blurred. The fins are not particularly noteworthy though the yellow tinted caudal fin usually has an attractive fan shape.

Breeding is not easy. A tank must be densely planted and a flower-pot is laid on its side and positioned so that the fish can enter and leave it easily.

Courtship and spawning arc along the usual lines and the rather large eggs are deposited within the flower-pot, or even under stones if the fish can gain access to them. The females must be removed when the spawning is finished, leaving the male to guard the eggs and fry until the latter are free swimming.

The fry will not need feeding for a couple of days after they have hatched, and it is then advisable to put them on to tubed food. They mature quickly.

Cardinal Tetra

Cardinal Tetra

Cheirodon axelrodi   CHARACIDAE
Original distribution: Brazil

This is the most beautiful of the 'tetras' and to some
extent has replaced the neon tetra (q.v.) as the most
popular of the more gaily-coloured fish.

The cardinal tetra is an excellent community fish,
being both peaceful and active, but to be seen at its
best it needs to be kept in a small shoal. It prefers soft
water in its tank and will grow to about 6.75 cm in
length. The fish is completely undemanding as
regards diet, but to keep it at peak fitness it should be
given an occasional live meal.

Male and female are very similar in appearance
but the latter is rather fuller in the body than the
male, though the species can be described as a slim
one. The body colouring is a reddish brown, and a
broad, brilliant red band runs from the mouth through
the eye to the end of the dorsal fin. Above this red
band is a fluorescent green band. The dorsal and anal
fins are colourless, apart from a narrow white edging
at the front.

Like the neon tetra this is not an easy fish to breed
successfully. It is advisable to watch the fish carefully

and select a pair that show a natural affinity. They should be separated and fed heavily on live food to bring them into condition.

The breeding tank must be densely planted at one end with a number of nylon breeding mops scattered in it. The female should be put in the tank in the morning and the male introduced at dusk. Spawning should take place early the next morning, evidenced by the fish darting into the plants and scattering semi-adhesive eggs.

The nylon mops with the eggs attached must be transferred immediately to a separate tank of the same temperature as the breeding tank. The tank containing the eggs must be left in total darkness and not examined for five days. The fry should then be free swimming and may be fed on infusoria or tubed fry food until they can take micro-worms and larger items of diet.

Checkered Dwarf Cichlid

Apistogramma ramirezi   CICHLIDAE
Original distribution: Venezuela

The species described below is the most common member of the genus *Apistogramma* to be found in aquarium tanks, though most have the description 'dwarf' as part of the common name. The dwarf cichlid, *Apistogramma agassizi,* from the Amazon is less peaceful and has smaller fins than the checkered dwarf; the body is yellowish towards the front and greenish-blue at the back, with yellow, bluish-green

Checkered Dwarf Cichlid

and black stripes in the caudal fin. The yellow dwarf cichlid, *Apistogramma reitzigi,* and cockatoo dwarf, *Apistogramma cacatuoides,* are less colourful varieties.

The checkered dwarf is not an easy fish to sex correctly. It is a shy, timid fish, growing to 6 cm and preferring a tank with plenty of hiding-places. Unfortunately, it tends to be a short-lived species.

The body is stubby and the fins (more especially the dorsal) relatively large; the front edge of the dorsal is black. The basic body colouring is purplish-red, covered with iridescent green or turquoise spots, but the colour changes with the light. When in spawning condition, the female develops a reddish colouring on both flanks.

For breeding, the checkered dwarf cichlid needs a tank with a sandy bottom, one end of which is densely planted, leaving plenty of free-swimming area at the other end. A few pieces of slate are scattered over the base of the tank.

The fish will clean the slate thoroughly before depositing the adhesive eggs. Although both parents will guard the brood (with the female usually taking charge), it is advisable to remove the slates to a separate tank when the eggs have been laid. Some of the eggs may fall on the leaves and should not be removed.

The eggs will hatch in three days at 26°C and the fry can be fed on infusoria, followed by sifted brine shrimp and micro-worms. Within a fortnight the fry can be fed on more adult food. The fish are fully mature at the age of six months.

Chocolate Gourami

Chocolate Gourami

Sphaerichthys osphromenoides　　BELONTIIDAE
Original distribution: Malaysia

The chocolate gourami is a delicate fish and is not really suitable for the inexperienced aquarist, for it readily succumbs to disease. If it can be nursed through its early troubles and becomes acclimatized to its tank, it is then quite hardy.

This fish needs a thickly planted tank and soft water at a temperature of between 26°C and 30°C. It is peaceful and usually quite at home in the community tank, but it must have a large percentage of live food in its diet.

There are no clearly recognizable differences between the sexes, and if breeding is to be practised, the brood fish should be selected on the basis of mutual attraction. The basic colouring is a dark brown, sometimes almost black, and the body carries four or five irregular bands of silvery-white. The dorsal, anal and pelvic fins are black, sometimes flecked with yellow. The dorsal fin is quite long but the anal fin is longer. The mouth is small and displays very small teeth.

The breeding habits of the species have caused some argument, but it appears that it is a bubble-nest builder. The male blows a number of bubbles to form a floating nest and mating takes place below it. As the fertilized eggs are dropped, the male takes them up in his mouth and spits them into the nest.

The female is removed once the eggs have been laid and their care then devolves on the male. He will keep the nest in repair by blowing fresh bubbles when needed. Additionally, he will aerate the eggs by brisk movements of the tail. An egg that falls from the nest will be replaced, but he is not as devoted a parent as most of the bubble-nest building breeds. The male can be removed when the fry are free swimming, and the young fish can then be fed in the usual manner.

Clown Barb

Clown Barb

Barbus everetti   CYPRINIDAE
Other name: *Puntius everetti*
Original distribution: Malaysia

The clown barb is a member of a very popular family
of aquarium fishes. Closely related species include
Barbus titteya (the cherry barb) and *Barbus nigrofasciatus* (black ruby), *Barbus conchonius* (rosy barb) and
Barbus schuberti (golden barb). The cherry barb
comes from Sri Lanka and grows to 5 cm, the male
being bright red with the female a lighter shade of
colour. The black ruby, also from Sri Lanka, is of the
same size, but is black in colour, though the front of
the male's body assumes a purplish tint during the
spawning season. The rosy barb's name suggests its
colouring and it is one of the largest of these barbs.
The golden-yellow golden barb is generally considered to be a hybrid species.

The clown barb is a good community fish, with a maximum size of 13 cm, and is one of the larger of the family. A temperature of 22°C is suitable.

The body colour is of a yellowish-pink, but it carries several blue or grey patches. The fins have a red tint in the male, but are more commonly pink in the female. The latter is larger and more full bodied than the male fish.

This is a difficult species from which to raise young. Conditioning of the prospective parents by heavy feeding with live food must be practised for three weeks prior to spawning, the male and female being put in separate tanks. The temperature of the breeding tank should be raised a couple of degrees and it should be planted quite densely.

As always, the female should be put into the breeding tank first, and should be given a day to get fully used to it. The male may be put in with the female overnight. Usually the ritual chasing is started by the female and is then taken over by the male. Spawning should take place within a few hours of the two fish being put together.

The eggs are scattered around the tank and a full spawning may take several hours. When it has obviously finished, the brood fish must be removed and the eggs left to hatch out. When free swimming, the fry can be fed on infusoria and finely sieved food. The fry mature rapidly.

The barbs are an important group of aquarium fish, and until the generic limits of *Barbus, Puntius* and *Capoeta* are resolved, all the barbs are placed in *Barbus*.

Clown Loach

Clown Loach

Botia macracantha   COBITIDAE
Other name: Tiger botia
Original distribution: Sumatra, Borneo

The clown loach is a useful scavenger for the
community tank as it is less nocturnal than most
loaches. It is a somewhat greedy fish with a liking for
small items of live food and thrives best in a water
temperature of 25°C. It needs hiding-places in its
tank.

Other *Botia* species include the tiger loach, *Botia
hymenophysa,* in variable colourings of green and
yellow with narrow cross banding, and the blue loach,
Botia modesta, which is of a greenish-blue colour with
yellow to reddish fins. All *Botia* species must be kept
in pairs, as a solitary fish is apt to become sulky and
then vicious towards other species.

The clown loach takes its popular name from the
three dark bands, one being from behind the dorsal
fin down to the anal fin, another in front of the dorsal
fin down to the belly, and the third passing from the

45

head to the eye. The basic body colouring is pale orange to a reddish-yellow, and the fins are red. The head is long and sharply pointed, the eyes are set rather high, and the fish has three or four pairs of barbels.

Little authentic information is available concerning the breeding of this fish in the aquarium, partly due to the fact that under such conditions it does not grow to its proper size. Some usually reliable sources report that the species has never been bred successfully in captivity.

Comb Tail

Comb Tail

Belontia signata   BELONTIIDAE
Original distribution: Sri Lanka

Owing to its decidedly pugnacious nature, this fish is not suited to the community tank. It has a rather chunky body with an arched back, and grows to a size of 7 cm. In spite of its aggressiveness, or perhaps because of it, the fish needs a tank with plenty of hiding-places. It cannot stand up well to cold conditions and a water temperature of some 2°C above the normal for a tropical tank is considered advisable.

The fish has been given its popular name because of the way in which the rays of the caudal fin extend some 3 cm to form the 'comb'. Apart from this feature it is not a particularly noteworthy fish, though its breeding habits differ from those of most of the members of its family. It does not make a bubble-nest, but its eggs float.

The male varies from greenish-brown to a darkish red on the back, changing gradually to a greenish-blue on the belly. Darker irregular bars are sometimes to be seen on the flanks, but the distinctness of these appears to depend on the condition of the fish. The female is smaller than the male and the colour is more of a uniform yellowish-brown.

A temperature of 29°C is suitable for the breeding tank and the prospective parents should be brought into condition by being kept in separate tanks and being fed heavily on live food.

The breeding tank needs to be planted quite densely and it is essential that floating plants also be put in the tank. The eggs are laid among these floating plants and a few bubbles blown by the male help to keep the eggs within bounds.

It usually takes the eggs some three days to hatch out and for the next 48 hours the fry will consume the contents of their yolk-sacs. They will then reach the free-swimming stage and must be fed on infusoria. The fry are not difficult to raise.

Congo Tetra

Congo Tetra

Micralestes interruptus   CHARACIDAE
Other name: Rainbow characin
Original distribution: River Congo

The Congo tetra is a peaceful species that extends its
fins strongly and has unusually bright and large eyes.
It does well in a tank having a temperature range of
23°C to 27°C. It is a fast-swimming species but one
that tends to keep towards the top of the tank, and it
is quite undemanding as regards food. The mature
male may grow to 7.5 cm, the female slightly less.

An unusual feature of this fish is that the central
rays of the caudal fin extend into a feathery shape, a
feature more pronounced in the males than in the
females. These appendages are often damaged but
will grow again.

The back is bluish and the rest of the body green,
the scales being opalescent. There is often a broad
yellow stripe along the side and sometimes shades of
gold and purple. The dorsal and caudal fins are
shapely.

Although this fish will breed in an aquarium tank, it is not easy to induce it to spawn. Perhaps the best method is to put the brood fish in a small tank and separate them with a glass panel so that they can see but not approach each other. While segregated they should be fed exclusively on live food.

The breeding tank should be large, well planted, and at a temperature of 25°C. The female should first be put in the breeding tank and the male some hours later, preferably overnight. The eggs will be laid among the plants, towards the bottom of them; the brood fish must be removed as soon as spawning is finished.

It will take almost a week for the eggs to hatch out at the temperature suggested. Compared with the fry of other species, those of the Congo tetra are large, with corresponding appetites. Almost from birth they will eat micro-worms and newly hatched (but sieved) brine shrimps.

Croaking Gourami

Trichopsis vittatus   BELONTIIDAE
Other name: Talking gourami
Original distribution: South-east Asia

This species differs from other 'croakers' in that the noise they make appears to be confined to the breeding period, and usually night-time. Both male and female make the sound.

The two important species are *Trichopsis vittatus*, growing to 6.5 cm, and *Trichopsis pumilus* (the dwarf

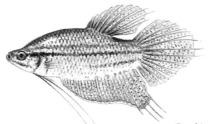

Croaking Gourami

croaking gourami) which becomes only 3.5 cm. Both are peaceful species, though active.

Tank temperatures need to be at the higher end of the range for this breed, a temperature of 28°C being suitable. These fish will accept almost any diet but show a preference for small items of live food.

Trichopsis vittatus is yellowish-green to a brownish shade on the back, merging into blue-white on the flanks and almost white on the belly; the flanks also carry longitudinal bands of a darker colour. One of the most uncommon features is that the fish has blue eyes. The male can be distinguished from the female by the longer anal and dorsal fins, the tips of the latter being slightly red.

The male of the dwarf croaking gourami is more vividly coloured than the female. The colour tends to be yellowish, tinged with green, and the darker longitudinal bands are also present. The fins are reddish.

This is not an easy fish in which to induce spawning, and while both parents help in the care of the brood they cannot be said to be entirely trustworthy.

A temperature of 30°C is needed in the breeding tank, the water-level of which needs to be reduced to 15 cm. Plants should be planted reasonably densely at one end only of the tank. The fish spawn in the normal way of the bubble-nest breeders.

The brood fish must be removed when the fry are free swimming, and if one of the parents is seen to be causing trouble before that occurs, it should be transferred to another tank immediately. The free swimming fry are brought to maturity in the usual way.

Croaking Tetra

Croaking Tetra

Glandulocauda inaequalis   CHARACIDAE
Original distribution: South-east Brazil, Paraguay

This fish lives and feeds towards the top of the tank. On occasion it will take a gulp of air and expel it as tiny bubbles through the gills, this process being accompanied by a faint croaking noise that has given rise to the popular name.

Although this is a small and peaceful fish that is quite at home in a community tank it is one that cannot tolerate undue temperature fluctuations, and the range of 20°C to 23°C represents the limits of its tolerance. This species will take all types of food and is an active, gregarious fish.

Another species of tetra is the blue tetra, *Mimagoniates microlepis,* which is a popular aquarium fish from Brazil. It grows to 7 cm and is silvery-blue in colour, the male being of a darker shade than the female. It has a broad blue lateral band.

The male and female of the croaking tetra can be distinguished with fair certainty on the shape of the dorsal fin which is pointed in the male and rounded in the female. Dorsal, caudal and anal fins are tipped with white, the body colouring is bluish, and yellow to dark green splashes of colour are sometimes seen in all fins.

The species is unusual in that fertilization of the eggs is internal. It is not a prolific fish and it is difficult to raise the fry. The breeding tank needs to be large, but the water shallow, the tank temperature being at 25°C. Heavy planting of the tank is essential.

Once spawning is complete it is advisable to remove the parents; the fertilized eggs should then hatch out within 72 hours. The fry are on the small side and need small infusorians once they are free swimming. Reports of successful rearing with tubed foods suitable for egg-laying breeds have been given. It will probably take ten days to a fortnight before the fry are really ready to take micro-worms.

Diamond Tetra

Diamond Tetra

Moenkhausia pittieri   CHARACIDAE
Original distribution: Venezuela

Diamond tetra is a useful species for the community
tank and when fully grown may measure between
5 cm and 7.5 cm. It is a fast-swimming fish and an
agile jumper. The diamond tetra thrives best in a
large tank, with a temperature between 21°C and
24°C. The tank should be thickly planted in one area
to provide hiding-places for the fish, though unfortunately the species shows a tendency to browse on the
plants. All types of fish food are accepted.

The body of the fish is silvery-grey or silvery-blue,
but this carries a large number of metallic coloured
spots which give attractive reflections under the light;
the eye is a vivid shade of red. The fish has a tall
crested dorsal fin and an unusually large anal fin.
The males are distinguished from the females by

their more pointed and longer anal, dorsal and pelvic fins.

Other aquarium members of the genus include *Moenkhausia oligolepis* (the glass tetra) from Brazil, this being yellowish with a black spot on the caudal peduncle, and *Moenkhausia sanctaefilomenae,* the red-eyed tetra. This fish originated in Paraguay and is of a nacreous yellow with dark edged scales forming a net-like pattern on the body. The male of the species grows to about 5 cm.

The diamond tetra does not breed readily when in captivity, and needs a water temperature for breeding similar to that of the community tank. The base should be covered with gravel, and fine-leaved aquarium plants should be anchored horizontally along the bottom. The brood fish should be introduced into the breeding tank overnight.

During courtship the male may be exceedingly aggressive. He drives the female vigorously over the plants where she will drop her eggs; these are immediately fertilized by the male. When spawning is finished the brood fish must be removed.

Eggs will normally hatch out in 48 hours, leaving the fry hanging on the plant leaves. In about three days they will become free swimming and will then take infusoria or very fine dried food.

Discus

Symphysodon discus   CICHLIDAE
Other names: Red discus, Pompadour, Disc cichlid
Original distribution: Amazon

Discus

In recent years this has become one of the most popular of the aquarium fishes. It is a timid species, not at its best in a community tank, but it thrives in a shoal of its own kind in a deep tank. This must be densely planted at the ends with ample clear space between so that the fish can be seen to the best advantage. It needs an almost exclusively live diet.

S. discus was the first of its genus to become widely known to aquarists and is still the most common, but other *Symphysodon* species are available and are sold under the name of discus. These differ from *S. discus*

55

only in their colouring, and they may be sold under such descriptions as the blue, green, brown, etc., discus.

The discus has an almost circular body which is laterally compressed. Although red is the predominant colour, this is liable to some variation according to the conditions in the tank. The pelvic fins hang down and swing back into a graceful curve. The body has several dark vertical stripes which change according to the condition of the fish, though the eye stripe remains visible. Sexing is difficult.

The fish may grow from 10 to 15 cm. Under certain conditions it will panic and will then become depressed and refuse food, though in normal health it can be regarded as rather greedy when offered live food.

Mutual attraction is the best way of selecting potential parents. The breeding tank should be shallow and a slightly acid water will encourage spawning; heavy planting of the tank is necessary. The eggs are adhesive and are laid on slate or flat stone which is carefully cleaned by the parents. The slate or stone should be propped firmly against the side of the tank. A broken flower-pot may also be used as a suitable repository for the eggs, 200 of which may be laid during the spawning.

It is unwise to leave the parents with the eggs for too long, for many brood fish will eat the eggs and even the fry if they are panicked. Some pairs, however, will care for the brood quite well. The fry grow rapidly after they hatch, which usually takes some 72 hours. The fry can be raised on routine lines and they will also obtain nourishment from the mucus of the parents' bodies, though not all brood fish are prepared to accept the attention of their young in this way.

Dwarf Gourami

Dwarf Gourami

Colisa lalia   BELONTIIDAE
Original distribution: India to Burma

This is a timid, hardy little fish that settles down quite well in the community tank. It is the smallest member of its genus, growing to 6 cm when fully mature, and is also one of the most attractive. It needs a well-planted tank with plenty of algae on which it can browse, and a water temperature in the region of 26°C.

The dorsal and anal fins are long in both sexes and are blue with a marking of red dots, the dorsal fin of the male being pointed when compared with that of the female; the pelvic fins are orange and drawn out. The body carries alternating red and blue bands. The caudal fin also carries markings of bands or dots.

57

Sexing is difficult though the male is usually the better coloured.

Two other members of the genus are commonly kept in aquarium tanks, the thick-lipped gourami and the giant gourami.

The thick-lipped gourami, *Colisa labiosa,* has nicely coloured fins and a silvery-green body with rather indistinct red bands. The mouth is best described as squat. Less timid than the dwarf gourami, the species needs a large tank. It is a native of southern Burma and is intermediate in size between the dwarf and giant gouramis, reaching a size of 8 cm.

The giant gourami, *Colisa fasciata,* has blue-green stripes on a brownish body with the belly and edge of the gill-covers green. Again, the fins carry attractive markings and colouring. The species is found in Bengal, Burma, Thailand and Malaysia. This breed may grow to 11 cm.

This is a bubble-nest breeder and it is reported that occasionally pieces of fine plant may be woven into the nest. Although nest-building is the male's responsibility, the female sometimes gives some help in the work. The behaviour of the male during courtship is dependent on his character. As a general rule he is reasonably gentle, but some specimens are aggressive and deaths have been reported from a too vigorous courtship. The female should be removed after spawning, followed by the male when the fry are free swimming. The fry are not difficult to rear.

Dwarf Pencil Fish

Dwarf Pencil Fish

Nannostomus marginatus   LEBIASINIDAE
Original distribution: Guianas, Amazon

Many species of slim, elongated fish are described as 'pencil fish', but this is one of the most popular for the aquarium.

It is a shy, slow-swimming and peaceful fish that prefers to be in the company of its own kind. It likes a tank that is heavily planted in some areas though with plenty of open swimming space. The dwarf pencil fish does well in a tank temperature of 24°C and, when fully mature, will measure some 3 cm. Although completely undemanding as regards the kind of food, this needs to be graded to suit the small size of the mouth.

Sexing of the species is not easy, but the males tend to be rather slimmer and are more brilliantly coloured. The body colouring is a brownish-grey, tending to be golden-brown along the back. Two darker brown stripes (which merge at the tail) run down the length of the body from the mouth and are separated by a gold band. The bottom and edges of the fins are reddish-brown.

A peculiarity of the genus is that when it is frightened, and often at dusk, the horizontal stripes

59

on the flanks of the fish vanish and are replaced by broad sloping bars.

There is also a less colourful brown pencil fish, *Nannostomus beckfordi,* from the Amazon with red fins. This has a dark horizontal band with an indistinct gold line above that merges into red.

The dwarf pencil fish does not breed readily. It needs a large breeding tank, preferably containing a breeding trap. The water should be at 24°C, and only 12 cm deep; slightly acid water is preferable. It is recommended that one male be mated to two females. The driving by the male is vigorous.

The eggs are scattered freely and the parents should be transferred when the spawning is finished. Hatching should be complete in 48 hours. Infusoria and flour-sized dry food are satisfactory first diets, these being followed by micro-worms, sieved daphnia and flake food as the fry mature.

Dwarf Rainbow Cichlid

Pelvicachromis pulcher   CICHLIDAE
Other name: Purple cichlid
Original distribution: Tropical West Africa

Several related species have been kept in aquariums but the species named above has proved the most popular.

It thrives in a large tank that is densely planted and has plenty of hiding-places. The fish are apt to be quarrelsome among themselves and, for a community tank, one compatible pair is preferable to a shoal. The

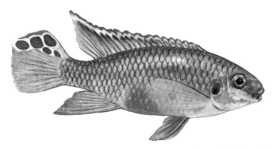

Dwarf Rainbow Cichlid

female will grow to 7 cm and the male to about 9 cm. They are lively fish, reasonably hardy, and will do well at normal tropical tank temperatures. Rainbow cichlids will browse on any algae present in the tank, but an occasional live meal is much appreciated.

The sexes are easily distinguishable for the female has a rounded tail, while that of the male is elongated and rather wedge-shaped.

The flanks of the fish are blue to purplish, sometimes with a definite purple spot, the back being of a brown shade; the belly is a dark colour, varying from red to purple, towards the caudal fin. Dark spots bordered with yellow are a feature of the caudal fin of the male, and these are usually in the upper part of the fin. The dorsal fin is attractively shaped and may have spots or bands of colour.

For breeding, the water temperature should be about 27°C. A flower-pot (with a small piece broken out of one side) is an ideal nest for the spawning, though plants must be provided and the aquarium base can be covered with sand. The courtship can be a rough affair. Normally the eggs will be laid within the flower-pot.

Many experts consider that the eggs should be removed to a separate tank for incubating. If the brood fish are left with the eggs the female may become aggressive towards the male, and it would be a sensible precaution to remove him.

The fry normally hatch out in 72 hours and less than a week later they will be free swimming and foraging for their own food. The rearing of the fry is along the normal lines.

Egyptian Mouthbrooder

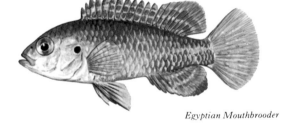

Egyptian Mouthbrooder

Hemihaplochromis multicolor   CICHLIDAE
Other names: *Haplochromis strigigena,* Small mouthbrooder
Original distribution: Egypt, East Africa

This fish is not recommended for the community tank even though it normally grows to not more than

7.5 cm. It needs a large tank, densely planted, and a water temperature of between 20°C and 24°C. Hiding-places in the tank are also necessary. This species accepts most fish foods, but live food should figure prominently in the diet.

There are other, less popular mouthbrooders such as the greyish-blue Nigerian species, *Haplochromis wingatei*, which has vertical dark bars, but these have not achieved the popularity of the Egyptian mouth-brooder.

As the scientific name of the latter suggests, the species is variable in colour. Usually the body colouring is a metallic green, but other colours from orange to blue are found on the flanks and also in the fins. These latter have rows of dots, sometimes black and yellow. The dorsal and anal fins are long.

Sexing of the fish is not too difficult. The female is noticeably heavier in the head and the anal fin of the male has a red tip. Colouring of the male is at its brightest when the fish is in a breeding condition.

The breeding tank needs plenty of oxygenating plants and a sandy bottom; the water temperature should be towards the upper end of the recommended range. With its caudal fin, the male sweeps a depression in the sand and the eggs are fertilized as they fall into this nest. The male must be removed as soon as the spawning is over.

The female picks up the eggs in her mouth and then refuses to eat until some time after the eggs have hatched. It may be almost a lunar month before the female can be removed from the breeding tank. The eggs will hatch inside the mother's mouth and, even when the fry are free swimming, the mother will gather them up in her mouth at the first hint of danger.

A recuperation period is important for the mother once she has been relieved of responsibility for the fry. Moreover, it is inadvisable to breed from the mother more than twice a year. The raising of the fry presents no special problems.

Firemouth

Firemouth

Cichlasoma meeki   CICHLIDAE
Other name: Firemouth cichlid
Original distribution: Guatemala, Southern Mexico

Several *Cichlasoma* species are kept in aquaria though the firemouth is probably the most popular.

The Jack Dempsey, *Cichlasoma biocellatum*, from South America is a pugnacious-looking fish with a big head, and may grow to 17 cm. The basic colouring is deep green with blue spots and the dorsal fin is edged with red. Also growing to a similar size is the striped cichlid, *Cichlasoma severum*, from the Amazon. This may show considerable variation of colour due to the mood of the fish, the basic colouring being dark green to almost black. Young fish show pale vertical bars, whereas the adults have a dark vertical stripe running from the dorsal fin into the bottom of the anal fin.

Both the preceding species are too aggressive to be kept in a community tank and they also root among the gravel and plants. The festive cichlid, *Cichlasoma festivum*, is more satisfactory in both respects, and is quite peaceable, though it needs a large tank as it may grow to 15 cm. Again, it is variable in colour but is usually of a shade of green and carries a dark stripe running from the upper tip of the dorsal fin to the snout, with vertical bars on the flanks and dark spots on the caudal peduncle.

The firemouth needs a water temperature of 23°C to 25°C. Only when small can it be kept in the community tank; it is a quarrelsome fish unless part of a compatible pair. It will eventually grow to about 10 cm. Some vegetable matter should be included in the diet. The fish are rather greedy eaters.

The sexes are not easily distinguished though the male has an elongated point at the back of the dorsal fin. The most prominent feature is the brilliant red colouring on the belly from the base of the tail right into the mouth. The body is bluish-green with irregular light purple markings and a dark broken line from the tail almost to the gill-plate. The colour of the fish is at its most brilliant when it is in a breeding condition.

This is quite a prolific fish and spawns in the same way as already described for other members of the family. It prefers to spawn on a piece of slate.

Firemouth Panchax

Firemouth Panchax

Epiplatys chaperi   CYPRINODONTIDAE
Other names: *Panchax chaperi*, Firemouth killie,
    Redjaw killie
Original distribution: West Africa

Although this is almost certainly the most popular member of its genus, there are other varieties well worth keeping in the aquarium tank.

Epiplatys annulatus grows to some 5 cm, the sexes being almost indistinguishable except that the female is less colourful. The species has four wide chocolate-brown bands on a yellow background, with red and blue tints in the caudal, anal and dorsal fins. It is popularly known as the clown killie.

The striped or banded killie, *Epiplatys fasciolatus*, has several dark vertical bars and a horizontal band on the sides. The back of the fish is brown with the flanks greenish, fading to silvery on the belly. It grows to 5 cm. Females of the species are lighter in colour. In general appearance it does not differ markedly from the firemouth, apart from the reddish colouring.

The large-spotted killie, *Epiplatys macrostigma*, takes its name from the irregular rows of large spots at the back of the body, the spots being reddish or brown.

The firemouth panchax is a handsome fish, easy to keep and peaceful. It needs a slightly alkaline water at a temperature of 24°C to 28°C. Community life suits it quite well. Live food must form the bulk of the diet though a little dried food may be taken.

Males can be distinguished from the females by their caudal fin which has a pointed extension, while the females are less brightly coloured and may have a yellowish throat. The colour on the back is dark brown, fading to light brown on the sides, with the throat and lower lip a vivid red. There are four to six dark vertical bars along the body.

Two females are mated to one male and they should be settled into the breeding tank before the male is introduced. The tank should be set out with floating plants as well as normal submerged ones. Spawning may take up to a week before completion, the eggs being laid and fertilized singly, up to a total of 20 a day. The eggs should be transferred to a separate tank and allowed to incubate under subdued lighting. Hatching will take approximately a fortnight.

Flying Barb

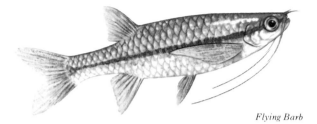

Flying Barb

Esomus danrica   CYPRINIDAE
Original distribution: Malaysia, India, Sri Lanka

In addition to the species described below there is a
Malayan flying barb, *Esomus malayensis*, which is of
similar appearance and habits, but has a black spot
near the bottom of the anal fin. It is smaller than
Esomus danrica.

The species takes its popular name from the wide
pectoral fins which enable it to jump with extreme
vigour, and as the fish keeps towards the top of the
tank, the temptation to jump is almost irresistible; a
covered tank is therefore essential. A large and thickly
planted tank is needed with a water temperature of
between 22°C and 24°C. Although not particularly
demanding as regards food, the flying barb needs a
certain amount of live food to ensure that it keeps
healthy. It will grow to a maximum size of about
9 cm. Food is taken at the top of the tank.

The genus has two pairs of barbels, one pair
sweeping well back towards the middle of the body.

In colour the fish is olive-green to a pale brown on the back, fading to a silvery-grey or silver on the flanks and belly, but under artificial lighting the body has a distinct violet sheen. The body also carries a dark horizontal line with a thin edging of a lighter shade, but as the fish ages this band tends to become blurred.

The sexes are difficult to distinguish, though the female is more rounded in the body and larger than the male.

For spawning a temperature of 26°C should be suitable. The tank must be thickly planted with submerged and floating plants. Spawning will actually take place among the floating plants, and the eggs will fall to the bottom as they are only semi-adhesive. As the brood fish may eat the eggs, a breeding trap is advisable, and the adult must be removed once the spawning act is finished.

Normally the eggs will hatch out within 48 hours, but the fry are often difficult to raise. After the yolk-sac is absorbed they may be fed on a tubed food, but as soon as possible they may be switched to a diet of minute live food.

Giant Danio

Danio malabaricus   CYPRINIDAE
Original distribution: Malabar Coast, Sri Lanka

The giant danio is a hardy, fast-swimming fish that may grow to 12 cm, being the largest of its genus. By aquarium standards it is a long-lived fish. It is peaceful enough to be kept in a community tank though the

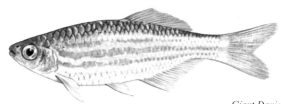

Giant Danio

inhabitants need to be chosen for size as the giant danio will scare small fish. A normal varied diet suits it quite well. Water temperature should be between 20°C and 25°C.

Sexing of the giant danio is not easy, but the lower jaw of the female does not protrude as much as that of the male, the colouring is less vivid, and the horizontal stripes are more broken. Additionally, the central blue stripe of the female tends to turn upwards towards the caudal peduncle.

The back of the fish is greenish to metallic blue and the belly slightly pinkish. The sides carry horizontal stripes of light blue, separated by yellow lines. The protruding mouth usually carries one pair of short barbels, though there may be a second, more stunted, pair. Fins show a reddish tinge when the fish is in a breeding condition, this colour often becoming quite intense. At non-breeding times the fin colour is lacking.

The female's body will noticeably swell as it becomes filled with eggs. A female showing such a swelling should be put in a breeding tank with a giant danio that does not show such swelling, for it will almost certainly be a male fish. Spawning, with the consequent fertilizing of the eggs as they are expelled by the female, should follow.

A large tank is needed for spawning and for this genus additional oxygenating plants or equipment is recommended. A reasonably heavy planting is desirable.

It is the female that customarily initiates the spawning and after the ritual display of fins, circling each other, and so on, the male starts to drive the female through the plants, with an occasional 'embrace'. The fertilized eggs are adhesive and very small and as many as 250 of them may be laid.

To save the eggs they should be removed to a tank of equivalent temperature, or alternatively the brood fish are removed immediately after spawning. The eggs will hatch within three days and care of the fry then follows along routine lines.

Glass Catfish

Glass Catfish

Kryptopterus bicirrhis   SILURIDAE
Original distribution: India, Thailand

This is a delicate species that takes food as it drops from the water surface. It is a reasonably good community fish but likes to be in a small shoal of its own breed in a water temperature of 25°C to 29°C. The glass catfish is timid and shy, and plenty of hiding-places should be provided in the tank. The preferred diet is small live food.

The glass catfish is considered to be the most nearly transparent of all aquarium fish and in certain lights it becomes almost invisible, but at other times the skeleton can be plainly seen. A prominent feature is the two long whiskers (barbels). Adult fish grow to about 6 cm.

There is a closely related species, *Kryptopterus macrocephalus*, known as the East Indian glass catfish, but this is rather less transparent and in certain lights it can be seen to have a bluish sheen. In both species the lower part of the caudal fin is slightly larger than the upper.

The East Indian species is the less gregarious of the two varieties, but in no case should a single specimen be kept as it is liable to mope and its health will then be seriously affected.

Glass catfish tend to have a habit of occasionally going to the bottom of the tank and resting motionless among the plants. While doing so, they may be slightly head downwards or even leaning to one side, giving the impression that they are dying or in poor health. This is quite normal behaviour, however, and they will soon dart away if disturbed.

A genuine sign of ill health is the appearance of black spots on the sides of the fish.

Little is known about the breeding characteristics of *Kryptopterus* and it seems that fry have not been raised successfully in captivity.

Glass Tetra

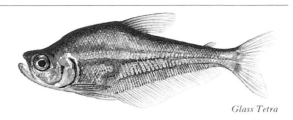

Glass Tetra

Roeboides microlepis   CHARACIDAE
Other name: Small-scaled glass tetra
Original distribution: Argentina, Eastern Brazil

Popular names often cause confusion in identifying a
fish and this is one example of it, for *Moenkhausia
oligolepis* may also be given the name 'glass tetra'.
Hence the alternative description of 'small-scaled'.

The fish is hardy but apt to prove quarrelsome at
feeding times. It needs a high proportion of live food
with its meals. Normal tropical tank temperatures
suit it very well. It is a species that tends to keep
towards the bottom of the tank where it swims head
downwards, though there is a clear distinction
between the appearance of this fish and that of the
fish known as 'headstanders'.

The glass tetra has an elongated body with a curved
back, small scales and a large mouth. When mature,
the fish may reach a size of 10 cm.

The basic colouring is yellowish, but under artificial
light small shiny dots can be seen; there is also a pale
green-blue stripe along the body. It is not, however, a
'glass' species in the way that certain fishes are, and

the air-bladder and skeleton cannot be seen. The fins have touches of colour in them, and in the case of the male this colour is likely to become intensified when the fish is in a breeding condition. The sexes are not easy to distinguish apart from the female being fuller in the body.

Breeding is far from easy and reports of successful spawnings are few. The tank needs to be a large one and courtship may be rough. The eggs are scattered and fertilized in the usual way of the Characidae. Because of their quarrelsome nature, only a compatible pair is likely to produce fertile eggs. Segregation and pre-conditioning may prove to be helpful.

Golden-eyed Dwarf Cichlid

Nannacara anomala   CICHLIDAE
Original distribution: Guyana, South America

In addition to the species described below, there is a lattice dwarf cichlid, *Nannacara taenia*, the male of which grows to 5 cm. This comes from the Amazon region. The colour tends to be somewhat variable from a greyish-brown to pale yellow, but there is a dark horizontal stripe that runs from the eye to the caudal peduncle, and above and below this stripe there are a few narrow lines. The lattice effect from which the fish takes its name is only apparent when the fish becomes excited, for vertical bars then appear on the sides. The care and breeding of the lattice dwarf is along the same lines as for the golden-eyed dwarf.

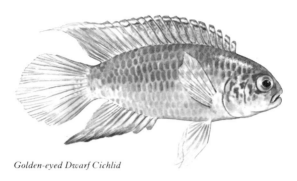

Golden-eyed Dwarf Cichlid

These dwarf cichlids make excellent community fish for they are peaceful and are not given to rooting among the plants or in the gravel. Normal tropical aquarium temperatures are suitable. The male attains a length of 7.5 cm, the female being smaller. Live food must form a high proportion of the diet, but freeze-dried foods and finely diced lean meats will also be accepted.

The body colouring is a metallic green or a brassy yellow, each scale having a dark spot. The dorsal fin is long, blue and edged with red and white. The throat and belly of the fish sometimes turn to a matt black shade when it is panicked or otherwise excited. The female has a pattern of dark stripes that cross each other to make a chequered pattern.

It is the female that normally takes the initiative in breeding, and at this time she may become quite aggressive towards the male. The eggs are usually laid in a flower-pot lying on its side.

Compatible pairs are essential for a successful mating, and segregation and conditioning of the brood fish are important. The very aggressiveness of the female and the timid reaction of the male are factors that mitigate against the raising of a brood. If the mating is successful, it will happen in the usual manner of the Cichlidae. The fry are not difficult to rear.

Golden Otocinclus

Golden Otocinclus

Otocinclus affinis   LORICARIIDAE
Other names: Dwarf sucking catfish, Otocinclus
Original distribution: South-east Brazil

There are other *Otocinclus* species and they are all small, excellent scavenger fish similar in practically all respects to the fish described below.

Like all the catfishes, this is a semi-nocturnal fish and though not a true 'upside down' cat it will occasionally assume that position immediately beneath the water surface; it will also rest on a leaf or something similar and adopt a most unusual posture. Unlike some catfish this species will do no damage to delicate plants provided that there is a sufficiency of other vegetable matter in the tank.

Although the otocinclus can be kept in a community tank it avoids bright conditions and it is necessary to provide plenty of foliage or dark hiding-places. It is not fussy about the water conditions and is capable of withstanding low temperatures as long as the tank is well oxygenated. This particular species will grow to about 4.5 cm, but other *Otocinclus* species may grow to twice that size. Any type of food is taken, but tubifex and vegetable matter is particularly relished.

The body of the fish is streamlined and dark brown on the back, getting pale in colour nearer to the belly, where it has a slightly darker mottling. In general the male is slimmer and a little smaller than the female. An extension of the lips forms a sucking organ. The fins are not outstanding and the members of the genus lack an adipose fin. As with all armoured catfish the body is protected with rough bony plates, and the head seems somewhat out of proportion to the rest of the body. The snout is pointed and the eyes moderately small.

Although something is known about the breeding habits of the species, it is not sufficient to recommend any special technique. Some breeding in tanks has been reported and it has been stated that the adhesive eggs were laid on the glass panels of the tank. Incubation took 48 hours.

Green Characin

Alestes chaperi   CHARACIDAE
Other name: *Brycinus chaperi*
Original distribution: Tropical Africa

Three species of *Alestes* have been imported, but it is the green characin that has gained the most popular-

Green Characin

ity. The other species have the same characteristics and requirements as the green fish.

The nurse tetra, *Alestes nurse*, is a relatively colourless fish that can grow to 23 cm. It must have a large tank and although it is not aggressive, it is unsocial and will have little to do with other fish, remaining in a shoal of its own kind. It needs a heavy diet of live food.

The long-finned characin *Alestes longipinnis* is of a silvery colour with fins that are reddish in the male and yellow in the female. The extended dorsal fin of the male gives the fish its most common name. Adult fish may reach a size of 12 cm.

The green characin is a lively and hardy fish and has a reputation as a jumper, so its large tank must be covered. It needs plenty of free swimming space but, being rather timid, it also likes planted areas in which to take shelter. Floating plants in the tank are appreciated. Normal tropical freshwater tank temperatures suit the fish well. Live food is essential and the fish soon becomes out of condition if it does not get enough of this. Fully grown adults may reach 10 cm. The green characin is less gregarious than the other species and it is not a particularly good community fish.

The body colouring is yellowish-green and the fish has a dark stripe along the middle of the caudal peduncle; the lateral line shows a distinct arch. The body is elongated and slim, and for its size the fish has a rather large mouth. The fins (which include an adipose fin) are slightly red in colour.

Although the fish can be assumed to breed by spawning, in the normal way of the Characidae, it would seem that it has never been bred successfully in captivity.

Green Rivulus

Green Rivulus

Rivulus cylindraceus   CYPRINODONTIDAE
Other name: Cuban rivulus
Original distribution: Cuba

Although the green rivulus has been taken as representative of the genus, many species have been introduced into aquarium tanks. They differ chiefly in colouring. A few of them are described below, but their characteristics, breeding, etc., are identical.

The golden rivulus, *Rivulus urophthalmus*, should be kept with fish of its own size. The male is brownish-green with longitudinal rows of small reddish dots along the side, the female being marbled and brownish. The 'rivulus spot', the false eye near the upper part of the caudal peduncle, and characteristic of the genus, is well marked in this species. There are variable colourings which have led to such descriptions as red or blue rivulus.

The rivulus spot is particularly striking in the eye-spot or ocellated rivulus, *Rivulus ocellatus*, in which the male is yellowish-green, its sides marbled with irregular dark blotches; the female is of a lighter shade.

Other varieties likely to be encountered are Hart's rivulus, *Rivulus harti*, the fire-tail, *Rivulus milesi*, yellow-banded, *Rivulus xanthonotus*, Santos, *Rivulus santensis*, and herring-bone rivulus, *Rivulus strigatus*.

The green rivulus is a peaceful fish, hardy, and an active jumper. It is one of the comedians of the fish tank and may adopt rather strange positions and hold them for some time. The rivulus is tolerant of a wide temperature range, but 22°C is a reasonable average figure. Floating plants as well as submerged plants are needed. Sometimes lethargic, the fish liven up considerably at feeding time and are not fastidious as regards the type of food.

In colour the green rivulus is olive-green, with darker green spots, and reddish spots towards the back of the fish. Sexing is simple, being indicated by the large rivulus spot and the drabber colour of the female.

Two females should be used for each male when breeding, the water temperature being raised to 26°C, and the tank being densely planted. The rivulus breeds freely and the eggs are widely scattered. The plants and fertilized eggs should be moved to a

separate tank for incubation. Eggs will hatch within
a fortnight, and for the first week of their life the fry
will need to be fed on infusoria.

Guppy

Guppy

Poecilia reticulata   POECILIIDAE
Other names: *Lebistes reticulatus*, Millions fish, Rain-
    bow fish
Original distribution: North-eastern South America

No other fish can challenge the popularity of the
guppy as the ideal fish for the beginner, yet cross-
breeding has resulted in new strains that satisfy even
the most advanced aquarist. One authority claims
that in the UK over 200,000 people keep this species.

The alternative common names provide some clue
to the popularity of the breed. It was called the
'millions' fish because of its prolific breeding habits
and the consequent great numbers in which it could
be found, and 'rainbow' because of the fantastic
combination of colours in which it is available.

Fancy guppies have been bred that concentrate on
the fins. Thus there are veil-tail, top sword, double
sword, scissorstail, round tail, lace- and delta tail

guppies, among a host of others. The guppy is tolerant of temperature changes provided that they are not too sudden; 23°C will suit the species admirably. Lively and hardy, this fish is undemanding with respect to food and will eat anything. It can also stand a greater degree of overcrowding than most species. Eight months after birth it is sexually mature.

The adult male rarely exceeds 2.5 cm in length. It is impossible to describe the colouring adequately for it can be any combination of red, yellow, blue, green, lilac, violet and so on, and often has darker markings superimposed on the background, and occasionally on the dorsal fin.

Sexing is simple for the female is silvery or silvery greyish-green, and may be twice the size of the male; it is also heavier in the body. The black gravid spot on the abdomen is strongly marked when she is ready to give birth.

The guppy breeds in the usual manner of the live-bearers. When at her peak, the female can produce a brood of up to 50 fry every month. It is advisable to remove the gravid female to a separate tank to have her young. The tank must be densely planted and provided with a breeding trap, for the parents invariably try to eat the young. When all the young have been born, the female should be removed to a tank of her own so that she will not be bothered by the male for a reasonable period. One fertilization by the male will result in several broods. The fry are easy to raise.

As with all live-bearers, a guppy will breed in a community tank, and some of the fry may escape the hazards of early life.

Half-beak

Half-beak

Dermogenys pusillus　　　　　　ExocoeTIDAE
Original distribution: East Indies

Although described as a peaceful species, the males
often stage mock combats that may scare other fish.
The species is unusual in that it has a fixed lower jaw
over which the upper jaw is clamped when the fish
feeds, which it does at the top of the water. It needs to
be kept in a covered tank. The half-beak creates some
problem in feeding as it will not accept dried foods.
The fish thrives best in a tank containing some
floating plants. Water temperatures of about 27°C are
advisable. The mature male has a body length of
7.25 cm, the females rather more.

There is a related species, *Dermogenys sumatranus*,
the Sumatran half-beak, which is very similar to the
fish described here.

The half-beak is instantly recognizable by the
extended lower jaw. The body is long and slim, olive-
brown on the back, fading gradually to pale olive on
the sides and finally to white on the belly. All fins
tend to be small, the caudal fin being slightly rounded,
and all have a reddish tint, this being most noticeable
in the pelvics. Sex differentiation is less easy than
with most live-bearers.

The male is sexually active, but successful matings
are relatively few. The females frequently miscarry

and many of the fry are stillborn. This is often the result of incorrect feeding.

For breeding, a thickly planted and shallow tank is recommended, and most authorities suggest that a slightly heaped teaspoonful of salt be added to every five litres of tank water. The female, in particular, has cannibalistic tendencies, hence a breeding trap is necessary.

The half-beak is a live-bearer. Neither male nor female needs conditioning for breeding, though a period of segregation may be helpful. Pregnancy lasts for about a calendar month, but the brood is likely to be small, and consist of only 15 to 20 young.

Rearing of the fry needs some care. When born, they are very tiny and the extended jaw does not develop for some weeks. Once the jaws develop the fish will need to be given live insects, but until that time infusoria and micro-worms, followed by sieved brine shrimp, will be appropriate feeding stages.

Harlequin

Harlequin

Rasbora heteromorpha   CYPRINIDAE
Other name: Rasbora
Original distribution: Malaysia, Sumatra

The harlequin has long been an aquarium favourite, but the *Rasbora* genus as a whole provides several other excellent hobby fish.

The spotted rasbora, *Rasbora maculata*, grows only to 2.5 cm. It is reddish-orange in colour, the male having a white belly, and has a round black spot on the side; the fins are reddish with black spots or markings. An alternative common name for the species is pygmy rasbora. A contrast in size is the elegant rasbora, *Rasbora elegans*, which may grow as large as 12 cm. It is silvery in colour, suffused with greenish or red-brown tints with a dark spot in the middle of the body and also on the caudal fin. The male of the species, usually clearly recognizable, has a yellow anal fin.

Intermediate in size between these varieties is the red-striped rasbora, *Rasbora pauciperforata*, which has a silvery body with a green sheen and a vivid red longitudinal stripe (bordered on the lower edge with black) along each side. One of the less common rasboras is *Rasbora leptosoma*. This has a horizontal stripe down the side, chiefly gold in colour but bordered with black and red at bottom and top respectively; the belly is white, and the back silvery, suffused with brown. The species is usually known as the gold stripe rasbora. The treatment of all species is the same as for the harlequin.

The harlequin is a peaceful community fish that prefers to live in a small shoal. Any kind of food is eaten. The most suitable water temperature is between 24°C and 27°C.

A striking feature is the dark wedge-shaped marking from halfway along the body to the tail. At the front the body is silvery, but it becomes suffused with pink as it nears the centre and this colour continues right through to the tail. The sexes are very similar, but the male is slimmer and more brightly coloured than the female.

Breeding is difficult. The female swims upside down and ejects her eggs against the underside of the plants. Up to 70 or 80 eggs may be deposited in a spawning that lasts two hours, but many eggs are lost. The parents should be removed after spawning and the eggs incubated in almost total darkness. When a successful hatching occurs the fry are not difficult to raise.

Headstander

Headstander

Chilodus punctatus　　　　　　　　CURIMATIDAE
Other name: Spotted headstander
Original distribution: Northern South America

Various genera have the popular name of 'headstander', but this is the most common and widely popular fish of that description. All such fish have the habit of adopting a head-down stance and will even take food in that position. Only rarely do they swim horizontally. The species described is the only one of the genus.

This is a slow-moving, peaceful fish that makes itself at home in the community tank. Live food and vegetable matter are essential to good health. It is a rather greedy fish and if given the chance will be continually nibbling. The species is small mouthed and food needs to be graded accordingly. Some hiding-places in the tank are necessary. A soft, slightly acid water is preferred, with the temperature at 25°C to 28°C.

The headstander is a comparatively colourless fish, but the attractively patterned scales in black, grey or brown give the fish a handsome appearance when viewed under certain conditions of lighting, and this is enhanced by an occasional silvery sparkle. The back is slightly arched and the belly rounded, the body being elongated. It has an adipose fin. Adult fish reach a size of some 7 cm.

It is impossible to sex the fish with any certainty, but the male is probably the slimmer of the two.

Reports suggest that on occasion this species has been bred in an aquarium tank, but this is a rare event because conditions must be absolutely perfect for breeding. The reports state that a large aquarium, sparsely planted and with a covering of floating plants is desirable, and it is also recommended that the tank should have a dark bottom. More work must be done with the species before recommended breeding techniques can be suggested.

Hunchbacked Limia

Hunchbacked Limia

Poecilia nigrofasciata   POECILIIDAE
Other names: Humpbacked limia, Black-barred limia
Original distribution: West Indies

There are several varieties of this delightful little livebearer, all of which need the same treatment as the hunchbacked limia.

The blue poecilia, *Poecilia caudofasciata*, comes from Jamaica. The body is covered with metallic blue spots, the belly of the male being rather yellow. Males have an orange dorsal fin with a dark coloured spot at the base. They are tiny fish, the male growing to 3.7 cm and the female to 5.7 cm. The green poecilia, *Poecilia ornata*, is slightly smaller but has luminous green dots and black spots, the latter also appearing in the caudal and anal fins.

The banded limia, *Poecilia vittata*, is not really banded because it has dark spots irregularly distributed over the yellowish-green background; the spotting is continued in some of the fins. The species originates in Cuba.

The hunchbacked limia is peaceful but active. A water temperature of about 24°C is suitable. Although it relishes the occasional live meal, algae and other vegetable matter form the greater part of its diet. Males will grow to 6 cm and the females slightly more.

Young fish show the arching of the back that gives this species its common name; this arching grows more pronounced as the fish ages. Similarly, colour changes occur with age. Juvenile fish are olive with a number of irregular dark bands, the belly being yellowish. A black edge develops on the belly of adult males and iridescent green spots are scattered over the bands. The dorsal fin grows larger, with its spines becoming black. In general the shape and colour of a really old fish is less attractive than the juvenile form.

The sexes are not easy to differentiate, but the colours of the female are rather more drab.

Breeding is along normal lines for live-bearer fish, but the fry are slightly less easy to raise than most of the type. It is helpful to put the breeding tank where it is exposed to natural sunlight.

Indian Algae-eater

Gyrinocheilus aymonieri GYRINOCHEILIDAE
Original distribution: Thailand

Like all loaches this species has a sucking disc by which it can anchor itself in any position it desires.

Indian Algae-eater

This ability is more useful in its natural surroundings than in an aquarium tank, as in nature it may need to hold its place in swiftly moving water currents.

As an aquarium cleaner this fish is unequalled for it will rasp off all algae with its sucking disc. In fact it lives almost exclusively on algae plus additional vegetable matter. It is a fish that needs a large tank with good aeration. While young fish are sufficiently peaceful, they become pugnacious as they grow older. Cases have been reported of the loach attaching itself to another fish and causing a wound (eventually resulting in the death of the host fish) when it pulls its sucker away.

A water temperature of 26°C is suitable and there must be plenty of plant life and algae. Feeding requirements have already been mentioned, but it may be noted that a small proportion of non-vegetable food will be accepted.

The fish can grow to a considerable size in the wild, but in the aquarium it is unlikely to exceed 17 cm. The genus is unusual in that it has an adaptation to the gill-covers that enables it to take in water through the gill openings (by which it obtains its oxygen) as well as expelling it, while it remains anchored to whatever it has attached its sucking disc.

The sexes are difficult to distinguish. The young fish are a uniform greyish-brown, with a lighter coloured belly. Dark blotches can be seen on the back, while the side carries an irregular dark stripe that may be broken up into short bars or blotches. The body is elongated with the back slightly arched. As the fish ages, its appearance and colouring change slightly.

Nothing is known about the breeding habits of this egg-laying genus.

Indian Glassfish

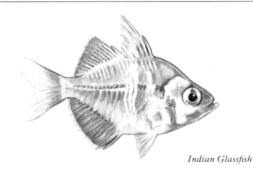

Indian Glassfish

Chanda ranga   CENTROPOMIDAE
Other name: *Ambassis lala*
Original distribution: India

This is a small species, rarely growing to much more than 3.5 cm. It is a hardy fish, but a well-established tank is preferable to one that has been newly set up, and slightly brackish water is also recommended. The Indian glassfish can accept a temperature of 18°C, but thrives better when the figure is nearer to 24°C.

The species settles down quite well in a community tank but cruises around in a small shoal of its own kind, so more than one pair should be kept in the tank. Because of its small size it can provide a meal for other fish when it is not fully grown, so the size of the other fish in the tank must be graded accordingly. Feeding of the Indian glassfish presents something of a problem as live food is essential, yet the fish cannot tear its food, which must be of a size that can be taken at one gulp.

The body is translucent but under the light it shows a pale yellowish tinge. Extremely fine, dark-coloured lines make vertical bars along the body. In strong light the air-bladder and skeleton can usually be seen clearly. The species has two dorsal fins, the second being soft. The fins are yellowish though the anal and soft dorsal fins of the male carry a blue edging.

Less commonly seen in the aquarium are the elongated glassfish, *Chanda nana*, and the Malayan glassfish, *Chanda buruensis*, both of which resemble the foregoing species.

The eggs are released and fertilized in the roots of floating plants in the breeding tank, the temperature of which should be raised to 25°C. Aquarium gravel is not needed. The number of eggs released is usually few and they remain among the plant roots. The brood fish do not normally eat the eggs or the fry, but it is preferable to release them from their parental duties as soon as the spawning is finished.

The eggs hatch out within 36 hours and the fry are free swimming after four or five days. They are not easy to rear. Infusoria are suitable in the early stages but small crustaceans (copepods) are essential once this stage has passed.

Jewel Fish

Jewel Fish

Hemichromis bimaculatus　　　　　CICHLIDAE
Other names: Jewel cichlid, Red cichlid
Original distribution: Tropical Africa

The fish is a savage species that will even attack members of its own kind; it is therefore not suitable for the community tank.

There is another species, *Hemichromis fasciatus*, which is much larger, more aggressive and less popular than the jewel fish. It is yellowish green in colour with a bronze sheen and five large and glossy black spots on each side. It is known as the five-spot cichlid or banded jewel.

The jewel fish needs to be fed on live food or scraped meat substitutes. A temperature range of 22°C to 24°C is satisfactory and a specialist tank should not be too heavily planted, as one of the fish's less attractive traits is the rooting up of plants. The fish is hardy. Adult males reach a size of 12 cm to 15 cm.

When not in breeding condition both male and female are rather dark in colour, with the body lined with blue jewelled scales; in breeding condition the fish change to a bright ruby-red, again jewelled both in the body and on the fins. An unusual feature is that the female is the more handsome fish at this time. The sexes are of similar appearance, but the male has larger metallic spots on its gill-covers and a crescent shaping of spots on its caudal fin.

Breeding of the jewel fish is not easy. The courtship is rough and if the female rejects the male, it is likely that she will be killed. Very dense foliage is needed for hiding-places in the breeding tank.

Spawning takes place on a stone or piece of slate that will be well cleaned by the female, or in a flower-pot laid on its side. To give easier access to the latter, the opening at the small end of the flower-pot should be enlarged. Both brood fish should be removed after spawning, although some breeders recommend that the female should be left with the eggs until they hatch, which they do in 72 hours after fertilization.

Care of the fry presents no unusual difficulties, but the jewel fish is one for the specialist and more experienced aquarist.

Kissing Gourami

Kissing Gourami

Helostoma temmincki　　　　　HELOSTOMATIDAE
Original distribution: Malaysia, Indonesia

This fish has a mouth of unusual shape which it puckers up when it is eating or sucking algae from the sides of the aquarium. Occasionally two fish will approach each other and remain locked mouth to mouth for a while, hence the name of 'kissing' gourami, though there is no reason to believe that the action has any real significance.

Although classified as a peaceful species, it is not suitable for the community tank for it can grow far too large (30 cm in the wild) and its very size can scare other fish; in the aquarium it rarely exceeds 18 cm. It will accept most foods but by preference it is a vegetarian. A water temperature of 24°C to 26°C is suitable. In its native haunts the kissing gourami is regarded as a food fish. It is a greedy species, needing several meals a day.

Juvenile fish that are sold may be of a pink colour, but the true colouring recognizable in adults is light greenish-blue to dark olive-green on the back, fading to silvery on the belly. The sides are marked with thin longitudinal wavy stripes and the caudal peduncle is crossed by a black bar. The lips are thick and protruding and the teeth are small. Dorsal and anal fins are both long, while the caudal fin is wedge-shaped. It is almost impossible to differentiate between the sexes in fish of aquarium size.

These fish will rarely breed in an aquarium tank, possibly due to the fact that aquarium-raised fish are insufficiently mature for the purpose, but even the larger specimens show some reluctance to breed.

A deep, well-planted breeding tank is necessary, with a temperature of 28°C. Kissing gouramis do not breed in the customary way of their family. After the routine courtship and chasing the pair embrace and the female will scatter up to about 50 eggs, which float to the surface. The eggs should be removed to a separate incubating tank where they will hatch in 72 hours. Spawning will continue until about 300 eggs have been laid.

The fry are rather large and need to be brought to maturity on infusoria and vegetable foods.

Kuhlii Loach

Acanthophthalmus kuhlii   COBITIDAE
Other names: Kuhlii eel, Snake fish, Coolie loach
Original distribution: N.E. India, Malaysia, Burma

Kuhlii Loach

This is a popular scavenger breed and its elongated snake-like body enables it to forage food from places completely inaccessible to other fish.

There are other species of *Acanthophthalmus* and all behave in exactly the same way, need identical treatment, and are sold as kuhlii (or, perhaps more correctly, 'coolie') loaches.

Although essentially a nocturnal fish the kuhlii loach, once it becomes acclimatized to its tank, can become quite active during the daytime. Some species can grow to 10 cm, but a more usual size for aquarium fish is 7.5 cm.

It is essential that the aquarium base be given a fairly thick layer of soft sand as these fish like to burrow on occasion, and when they are kept in a tank confined to their own kind good aeration and shallow water is recommended. Such a tank should be sparsely planted and kept fairly dark. There is no reason why kuhlii loach should not be kept in a community tank, for they are peaceful enough.

A tank temperature of 24°C to 28°C is suitable. In the community tank kuhlii loach will consume food ignored by the other fish, though they also appreciate the occasional live meal. Living and feeding at the bottom of the tank as they do, the fish will also occasionally adopt an odd resting posture on the plant leaves. They swim with an eel-like motion and it is worth noting that they are not easy fish to net.

The cylindrical body is elongated and carries 15 to 20 regular dark stripes across the back, though these are broken on the belly of the fish. The body is covered with minute scales. A transparent film covers the small eyes and in front of each eye is a small spine that can be raised. The mouth is directed downwards and is furnished with three pairs of barbels. The fins are insignificant. It is impossible to differentiate between the sexes.

The genus is exceedingly difficult to breed and apparently it has not yet bred in an aquarium. It is believed that in the wild this species breeds in open water, and is possibly a bubble-nest breeder.

Lamp Eye

Lamp Eye

Aplocheilichthys macrophthalmus CYPRINODONTIDAE
Other name: Lantern eye
Original distribution: Lagos

Other species of the genus are occasionally kept in an aquarium tank, but the one described below is the most popular. It takes its common name from the eyes, which are exceptionally large for the size of the fish. In subdued light these eyes reflect gold-green.

The lamp eye is a small and active fish that must be kept in a covered tank as it is a great jumper; floating plants may help to restrain this tendency. It is a hardy fish with a liking for a well-established tank and a temperature of from 23°C to 26°C. Small items of live food are taken avidly, but all types will be accepted, particularly if they contain ground shrimp, etc.

Mature fish rarely grow to more than 3 cm and in view of this it is unwise to keep them in a tank in which more predatory species are accommodated.

The fish has a slightly flattened head and a mouth opening that is slanted slightly upwards. The body is elongated and, at the front, is slightly compressed laterally. In colour the species is a translucent greyish-green, the colour being paler on the body. There is a dotted metallic line down the side and a narrow dark stripe may also run down the back. The fins are rather attractive, the caudal, dorsal and anal having a pale blue tinge; pale red dots may also be present in the caudal fin.

The sexes are distinguishable by the fins, as the dorsal and ventral fins are less pointed in the female than in the male.

In breeding, the female does not scatter her eggs. They may be laid singly, or alternatively in small clusters that dangle from the vent of the female until being brushed off against the plants. Normally the brood fish do not eat the eggs, but it may be wiser to transfer the parents to a separate tank.

The eggs will usually hatch out in about ten days. The fry are rather delicate and they need a great deal of attention if they are to be raised to maturity.

Leaf Fish

Leaf Fish

Polycentropsis abbreviata   NANDIDAE
Other name: African leaf fish
Original distribution: West Africa

This is most certainly a fish for the specialist. It is a small but vicious predator that will even attack its own kind. The common name comes from the appearance of the species which is brownish in colour and has an almost invisible tail, so that it resembles a dead floating leaf until the time comes for it to snap into action.

Another leaf fish, *Polycentrus schomburgki*, comes from South America and Trinidad, but it is rarely seen in an aquarium. It is known as Schomburgk's leaf fish and while not of the same genus as the leaf fish described here, it is closely related to it. The colour is light brown to bluish-black, with a silvery glint and darker spots. It grows to 5 cm.

A soft water is best for the leaf fish and also subdued lighting, as the species is largely nocturnal. Plenty of plants are necessary as the fish likes to stay at rest among them for fairly long periods. The diet consists of chopped earthworm, fresh chopped heart and other animal organs, and all live foods. The temperature range is 25°C to 28°C.

The sex of the fish cannot be determined with certainty. Adult fish grow to 3.75 cm. The head is large and the mouth extremely wide. The colouring is yellowish to brown, marbled with darker tints. The body colouring extends into the fins, except for the caudal fin which is transparent.

Floating plants and debris must be put into the breeding tank, with soft sand on the base. The temperature should be held steady at 28°C.

A bubble-nest is built on the underside of the debris and up to 100 eggs are ejected into it by the female, who is in an inverted position. She must be removed after spawning, but the male must be left until the fry are free swimming. The eggs hatch in 48 hours and the male then transfers them to a small depression that he fans in the sand. The fry are extremely voracious and grow quickly.

Lemon Tetra

Hyphessobrycon pulchripinnis   CHARACIDAE
Original distribution: Amazon basin

The lemon tetra is an exceptionally well-behaved fish in the community tank, but is at its best when it forms

Lemon Tetra

part of a small shoal of four or six. It is lively, alert and hardy, as well as being peaceful. The lemon is one of the best of the tetras and probably ranks next to the neon in popularity by those aquarists who keep these fishes.

A water temperature of between 22°C and 26°C suits it best, and it likes a tank with plenty of open space in which it can display its swimming prowess. It will accept all types of food but should be given an occasional live meal to keep it in good health. Adult fish rarely exceed 5 cm in size.

The difference between the sexes in general appearance is only slight, and although the male may be the slimmer of the two, this factor is not always a reliable one. Breeding is therefore tried with pairs that have shown a mutual liking.

Lemon tetras have somewhat transparent bodies that reflect silver with a faint tinge of yellow. The anal fin is a deeper shade of yellow in the first few rays, with a deep black stripe and black streaks along the bottom edge of that fin; the anal fin has a more clearly defined triangular shape than is customary with most species. The front rays of the dorsal fin are black with bright yellow tips. The upper part of the eye is a brilliant red, the lower part being yellow.

It is not easy to ensure a successful mating with this species, and it is essential that the pair be compatible.

The female must be well-conditioned beforehand. The breeding tank should be shallow, with a water depth of 15 cm and a temperature of 26°C; no gravel should be laid on the base of the tank. Dense planting is recommended.

When introduced into the breeding tank the male will go into the ritual courtship dance and coax or drive the female into the plants. A few eggs will be laid each time this happens, but as the brood fish are inveterate egg-eaters only a few of them will survive. The brood fish should be removed when the spawning is over.

The eggs should be allowed to incubate in subdued light and the fry will be raised easily on normal feeding techniques.

Leopard Corydoras

Corydoras julii   CALLICHTHYIDAE
Other name: *Corydoras leopardus*
Original distribution: East and North-east Brazil

The genus *Corydoras* provides the most popular of the aquarium catfish, though the requirements and care of all of them are along the lines described for the leopard corydoras. Some of the species are, however, worthy of mention.

The bronze corydoras, *Corydoras aeneus*, from Venezuela and Trinidad is bronze green with no

Leopard Corydoras

distinctive markings; it grows to 9 cm. The blue corydoras, *Corydoras nattereri*, is smaller (6 cm) and silvery-brown with a translucent blue overtone, while the peppered corydoras, *Corydoras paleatus*, is yellowish with irregular dark blue markings and occasional green scales. It grows to 7.5 cm.

Corydoras arcuatus (the arched corydoras), growing to 5 cm, has a whitish body with a mauve sheen and a dark stripe curving from the eye to the caudal peduncle, while the spotted corydoras, *Corydoras punctatus*, is pale brown with dark spots on the side; it grows to 6 cm.

The catfish is an excellent scavenger and a good community fish. It likes hiding-places in a tank of normal tropical tank temperature, but it is tolerant of a wide range of temperature conditions. These are active, long-lived fish, and will eat almost anything.

The leopard corydoras is whitish-grey in colour with the head and upper half of the body well peppered with numerous black spots which tend to form three lateral lines along the body. The caudal fin has a number of almost symmetrical spots and the dorsal fin may show a black spot towards the top. Sex differentiation is not easy, but the male has longer, more pointed, pelvic fins than the female, and is also slightly smaller.

Leopard corydoras do not breed readily in captivity and most experts believe that three to four males should be used with each female. The breeding tank must be supplied with flat stones or pieces of slate on which the female can deposit her eggs; she will clean these thoroughly before laying. The courtship can be attractive to watch, and it is the female who will make the first advances. Only a few eggs are laid at one time, and if given the opportunity the brood fish will eat them.

The eggs will normally hatch in three to four days and the fry can then be raised fairly easily.

Lyretail

Lyretail

Aphyosemion australe   CYPRINODONTIDAE
Other name: Cape Lopez lyretail
Original distribution: Gabon

The lyretail is not the only member of the genus to be kept in the aquarium but it is the most popular. Other species may be sold as red, blue, etc. lyretails.

The blue and yellow gularis, *Aphyosemion coeruleum* and *Aphyosemion gulare* respectively, are active, carnivorous fish, as is the banded fundulus, *Aphyosemion bivittatum*, but all lack the attractive caudal fin shaping of the lyretail.

The lyretail is a good community fish, thriving in slightly acid, well-matured water in the tank. It will take the occasional dried meal but prefers a live diet; it is a hearty feeder. Normal tropical tank temperatures suit it well. It grows to some 7 cm.

The male is the more handsome fish. In colour it is a dark brown on the back, gradually fading to bluish-green on the body, with irregularly spaced and shaped red spots on the flanks. The long flowing anal and dorsal fins have an edging of carmine with stripes of blue. The lyre-shaped tail has a bluish-green centre with carmine dots. Around this is a broad carmine stripe with white tipped orange or pink outer rays. The female is relatively plain.

When mating, male and female lie side by side, trembling vigorously. During this time a single egg is laid which the male fertilizes. As many as 100 eggs may be laid, scattered among the plants, hence the spawning will continue over several days.

The eggs take a long time to hatch, sometimes up to three weeks, and although the brood fish are not likely to eat the eggs, it is advisable to transfer the latter to a separate tank for incubating.

The fry are not difficult to raise, provided that they are started on infusoria and gradually weaned to more adult food. Breeding and rearing will be facilitated if the temperature of the breeding tank is raised not more than 2°C above the normal tank temperature.

Madagascar Rainbow Fish

Madagascar Rainbow Fish

Bedotia geayi　　　　　　　　　ATHERINIDAE
Other name: Madagascar minnow
Original distribution: Eastern Madagascar

This is a peaceful and hardy little fish that prefers the upper part of the tank and will not leave it in pursuit of its food. It grows to a maximum size of 8 cm, and although it has not been known to aquarists as long as some species, it is a well-established favourite.

The genus is somewhat unusual in that its members have two dorsal fins, the first having a short base and the second a long one. A lively swimmer, *Bedotia* is at its best in a small shoal and at a fairly high water temperature, say 25°C to 28°C. The Madagascar rainbow is a good community fish and will accept a mixed diet quite happily.

Sexing of the fish is not too difficult, the male being more deeply coloured than the female and having the end of his caudal fin coloured red.

The basic body colouring is greenish-olive and the sides carry a dark longitudinal stripe that runs from the eye to the caudal peduncle. Vertical fins are bordered with a dark edging and are tinted yellow, while the fins of the male may show red patches, the colouring at the tips of the caudal being standard for the genus.

It is a relatively easy species from which to breed and is one that needs a rather hard water. The temperature of the water should be a minimum 26°C and the tank should be densely set out with submerged plants.

The male takes the mating initiative by driving the female through the plants. Spawning lasts for several days, only a few large eggs being deposited each day. The eggs hang by a short filament on the plants and in most cases are ignored by the parents.

The eggs will hatch in about a week, but it should be noted that as a result of the prolonged spawning the fry will be at different stages of development. When free swimming they remain near the surface of the water. Dust fine dried foods and newly hatched brine shrimp are accepted at a very early age.

Marbled Headstander

Abramites hypselonotus　　　　　　　ANOSTOMIDAE
Other names: Headstanding fish, Norman's head-
    stander
Original distribution: Lower Amazon

This headstander is one of the less common aquarium fish and takes its name from the manner in which it swims, with the front part of the body downwards. This is quite an eye-catching feature. In spite of its unusual posture, the fish does not feed from the bottom of the tank.

Marbled Headstander

Small specimens of the marbled headstander cause no trouble and can be left safely in a community tank. Care must be taken, however, for as they get larger they sometimes turn aggressive towards smaller fish. A size of 7.5 cm to 12.5 cm may be attained in an aquarium. These fish cannot bear cold water and a minimum temperature of 24°C is essential, though they are not fussy about the nature of the water. A densely planted tank with plenty of hiding-places is preferable. The species is undemanding as regards food, but it must be given a reasonable amount of vegetable matter.

A marbled headstander has an arched back and a tiny head, which is rather pointed; the body is slightly elongated. Colour tends to be variable from yellow to a red-brown, with dark vertical bars on the side and a marbling of grey to brownish colour. The caudal fin is marked with a white crescent. The adipose fin is not large. The headstander almost invariably looks at its best when in a small shoal of its own kind.

Reports suggest that the fish has been bred successfully in aquarium tanks, but only on rare occasions, and there is no authentic information about its breeding habits. Presumably they are the same as for the other members of this oviparous family. No advice can therefore be given as to how best to practise controlled breeding.

Medaka

Medaka

Oryzias latipes   CYPRINODONTIDAE
Other names: Rice fish, Geisha
Original distribution: Japan, China, Korea

There are four species of *Oryzias* and these may all be sold under the name of medaka, but it is the one described in detail below that is the most important. The black-spotted medaka, *Oryzias melastigma*, comes from India and Sri Lanka and has several dark spots on the sides. The Celebes medaka, *Oryzias celebensis*, and the Java medaka, *Oryzias javanicus*, differ little from *Oryzias latipes*. The Javanese species is occasionally sold as the Java killie or Java rice fish.

Oryzias latipes is an excellent community fish and is capable of withstanding a considerable variation of water temperature providing that the change is not too abrupt; a temperature of 20°C to 24°C is about right for the fish. They are not the least fussy about their food and will eat anything reasonable that is given to them.

The body is slightly elongated and the head flattened. They are almost transparent in their original form, but have now been bred to an attractive golden colour. They carry no distinctive markings. The normal size for a fully grown adult male is 5 cm, the female being slightly larger. Differentiation of the sexes is difficult, though the males have slightly larger and better shaped fins.

Breeding is not difficult if the tank is well planted with fine-leaved and floating plants. Courtship is occasionally rough. The amber tinted eggs hang from the vent of the female until they have been fertilized.

If the brood fish have been properly conditioned and there are sufficient plants in the tank to provide enough hiding-places, they may not molest the eggs or the fry, but it is a wise precaution to remove all plants carrying fertilized eggs to a separate incubation tank.

The eggs will usually hatch out within a fortnight and the fry can then be removed and reared first on infusoria, followed by dust fine sieved dry food, and finally micro-worm and other more adult foods.

Merry Widow

Phallichthys amates   POECILIIDAE
Original distribution: Belize, Guatemala

This is a long-established aquarium favourite, not to be confused with the black widow described earlier.

Merry Widow

There is another member of the genus, *Phallichthys pittieri*, which differs from the merry widow chiefly in colour and size. It is pale olive-green with dark bars on the sides of the male, and the sides reflect a blue sheen. In both varieties a noticeable feature is the long gonopodium, slightly hooked at the end, which reaches as far back as the caudal peduncle.

The most suitable temperature range for the merry widow is 21°C to 25°C. It is a lively fish, excellently behaved in the community tank, and is reasonably hardy, needing only the normally planted tank. The breed likes green algae and vegetable matter, and will take dried food avidly.

Male and female are readily identifiable on account of the gonopodium alone, but other factors are that the female grows to twice the size of the male, lacks the characteristic marking of the male dorsal fin and also the coloured bars.

The adult male grows to 3 cm. It is olive-green in colour, with dark vertical bars (up to twelve in number) on the side, and a short black line passing through the eye. The gills are blue. The particular feature that has given the fish its popular name is the handsome dorsal fin which has a thin black edging giving it a fanciful resemblance to an old-fashioned mourning card.

The merry widow is quite a prolific breeder but it is apt to eat its young. No breeding tank is necessary, nor is any special treatment required, for this species will breed happily in the community tank. If the tank contains a breeding trap the young can be raised without difficulty. At birth the fry measure 0.6 cm, but they grow rapidly.

This fish is viviparous, and one fertilization will result in several broods. Pregnancy may last up to six weeks. At her peak the female may lay up to 100 young, but many of these will not even be lucky enough to find their way into the breeding trap.

Molly

Molly

Poecilia sphenops   POECILIIDAE
Other name: *Mollienesia sphenops*
Original distribution: Central America

No community tank could be considered complete without specimens of the 'molly'. After the guppy it is almost certainly the favourite fish of the beginner and the number of species is such that a large tank could be devoted to them and still not include them all.

A water that is slightly alkaline is suitable and this must be at a temperature of from 23°C to 28°C. The fish have a great liking for algae and other vegetable matter, but the diet should include all forms of dried and live food, which will be accepted without quibbling. According to species, a fairly large tank may be needed and if breeding is to be practised on general, rather than controlled, lines a breeding trap must be installed, for to move a gravid female can result in miscarriages and possibly the death of the mother.

The marbled molly, *Poecilia sphenops*, provided the original stock from which various strains have been 'line bred' and this original species is rarely seen in the aquarium. The most popular variety is undoubtedly the black, perma black or midnight black molly, which resembles a scrap of black velvet swimming among fish of brighter hues. A most attractive fish, it does not always breed true. All fry are silvery mottled with black spots, and some of these will later develop all-black colouring while others remain mottled.

The sailfin molly, *Poecilia latipinna*, takes its name from the gorgeous dorsal fin of the male, for this is iridescent blue, may be taller than the body of the fish, and can extend the full length of the body. The caudal fin is pale blue with a yellow streak. The fish grows to 9 cm.

The giant sailfin molly, *Poecilia velifera*, grows to a larger size than the sailfin and has an even larger dorsal fin patterned in brown, red, blue and orange, with the latter tint showing on the throat.

Pure black mollies are also bred from the sailfin and giant sailfin, together with lyretail and other fancy breeds. The fins of the species are displayed at their best during courtship, and when several males live in one tank there is some possibility of fin damage if they decide to fight. Similarly, in a community tank that contains tail-nipping species, these latter will find the temptation irresistible.

A female molly will become mature at eight months and over a two-month period can produce up to 100 fry. The males are particularly virile and must be mated to several females. Brood fish almost invariably show cannibalistic tendencies. Controlled breeding is done along the normal lines for live-bearing species.

Mosquito Fish

Mosquito Fish

Heterandria formosa   POECILIIDAE
Other name: Pygmy live-bearer
Original distribution: North Carolina, Florida

A peaceful fish, and the smallest of the live-bearers, it is unlikely to last long in the community tank. Fully adult males rarely grow to more than 2 cm and the females are only slightly larger. The fish thrive in normal tropical tank water temperatures, and are agile when in shoals. They like occasional live meals, though these need to be graded for the size of the fish.

The mosquito fish takes its common name from the fact that it is one of the many that have been used to control mosquitoes by eating the larvae.

As with all live-bearers, the male can be distinguished from the female by its modified anal fin which is, in effect, a sexual organ.

In colouring, the back is a deep brown with the sides brownish-olive and the belly silvery white. Along the side is a dark horizontal stripe that has eight to twelve dark bars crossing it. The dorsal fin carries a red spot. The mouth opening is small, even bearing in mind the size of the fish, and it is tilted upwards.

There is a slight difference in the manner of the breeding of these live-bearers as compared with others of its kind, as the births are staggered over a number of days.

If properly fed, the female will be pregnant every fourth or fifth week. Normally a special breeding tank is not required and provided that the tank is densely planted and that some form of breeding trap is installed, the mosquito fish will breed readily in its own tank. However, the survival rate among the fry will almost certainly be low.

To ensure that the fry stand a reasonable chance of survival, and to raise them under the best possible conditions, the female should be transferred to a separate tank as soon as the gravid spot can be seen, and she will then give birth to one, two or three young every day over a period of about 14 days. Possibly 25 live births will result over the period. It is vital not to remove the female until after 10 or 12 days from the first birth to ensure that all the young have been born.

The mother must never be handled near to her delivery time, otherwise premature births may occur.

The fry will be at different stages of development and consequently their food requirements will vary.

Mozambique Mouthbrooder

Mozambique Mouthbrooder

Sarotherodon mossambicus   CICHLIDAE
Also known as *Tilapia mossambica*
Original distribution: Eastern Africa

This is a commonly kept cichlid, and is particularly suitable for a large tank as it grows to a length of about 35 cm in the wild, and usually up to c. 20 cm in a home aquarium.

Except during the breeding season the male and female are silvery grey or greenish. As spawning time approaches the female remains more or less the same but the male develops an attractive blue coloration on the flanks, becoming rather darker along the back.

The most striking feature, however, is the brilliant red edging to the dorsal and anal fins.

Like related cichlids this is a heavily built fish with a big head. If possible it should be kept as a small group in a large, spacious tank, as it grows very rapidly. It likes to burrow so the substrate should be gravel and, of course, there should be no rooted plants as these would soon be dug up. The tank can also have a few firmly positioned rocks and old roots to provide shelter. It is also a good idea to have a few floating plants to cover part of the water surface; these will give areas of shade. It is fortunate for the aquarist that this hardy cichlid requires no special water conditions. In the wild, in fact, it frequently enters the brackish water at the mouths of rivers and in the aquarium it has even been known to breed in water that is 50 per cent salt and 50 per cent fresh water.

The diet also presents no problems, for the Mozambique mouthbrooder will take live food, such as insects, worms and small crustaceans, as well as chopped meat and the usual dried foods. A certain amount of plant food such as blanched lettuce or spinach will also be appreciated.

Many cichlids practise brood protection and the Mozambique mouthbrooder is one of the best examples. The male digs one or more pits in the gravel and spawning takes place in one of these. As soon as the eggs have been laid and fertilized they are taken up into the female's mouth. There they remain for about 9–12 days before hatching into tiny fry which still continue to be protected by the female for some time, swimming around close to her body. They have often been seen to retreat into the female's mouth at night or when threatened. Gradually the fry move away and start to lead an independent life.

The Mozambique mouthbrooder is not only an interesting cichlid on account of its breeding habits, but it is also important as a source of human food. For this reason it has been introduced into several parts of the tropics, as for instance Malaya, where it is successfully bred in scientifically controlled fish ponds.

Neon Tetra

Neon Tetra

Paracheirodon innesi   CHARACIDAE
Other names: *Cheirodon* or *Hyphessobrycon innesi*
Original distribution: North-east South America

This is an excellent community fish if it is kept in a shoal of six or more and is not put with other fish of too great a size. It grows to about 4 cm, is hardy and peaceful, and until superseded by the cardinal tetra was one of the prime aquarium favourites.

The neon is not the sole representative of small tetras. Other popular species include *Hyphessobrycon flammeus* (the flame fish), which is silver suffused with pink, the dawn tetra, *Hyphessobrycon eos*, of a delicate gold, and the dwarf tetra, *Hyphessobrycon minimus*, of a silvery-grey colour, but these all lack the distinctive colouring of the neon. The popular name of tetra is not, however, confined to *Hyphessobrycon* species.

A water temperature of 20°C to 25°C suits the neon tetra well. It will eat very small live food or fine dry food; freeze dried food has also proved acceptable.

The distinctive feature of the neon is the luminous blue and green stripe that runs from the snout through the eye to the adipose fin, and a vivid red splash of colour running from the base of the pelvic fin to the caudal peduncle. It is a slender fish with a small mouth. Sex differentiation is difficult, the male being only slightly slimmer than the female.

It is still considered to be something of a feat for an amateur to breed the neon tetra. One method that has produced successful results is to use a slightly hard water in a normal breeding tank, the water being absolutely clear. The tank should contain no gravel. The breeding fish should be young, and if possible a compatible pair. Spawning should take place in the early morning, 150 to 200 eggs being laid. The adults must be removed immediately and the tank darkened.

A little light should be let into the tank after five days, when the fry will be free swimming, and this amount should be very gradually increased. Infusoria are not given as the fry will take tiny live food, provided several times a day. The tank must be kept scrupulously clear of uneaten food, etc. If the fry survive their early days, they will grow quickly.

One-striped African Characin

One-striped African Characin

Nannaethiops unitaeniatus   CITHARINIDAE
Original distribution: Equatorial Africa

This is a peaceful, hardy, but rather shy fish though
it settles down readily to life in a community tank. It
is not fussy as regards diet and is tolerant of a wide
range of tank temperatures; an average temperature
of 23°C will suit it admirably. The breed has good
erect fins and these, with the attractive colouring, are
displayed at their best only when the tank conditions
are correct.

Although there is little colour differentiation
between the sexes the male is the brighter of the two,
while the female is higher in the back and plumper.
Mature males grow to 6.5 cm and the females to
7.75 cm.

The fish has a dorsal fin the front edge of which is
edged with black; in some specimens splashes of red
may also be present in this fin. The upper part of the
body is dark brown to brownish-red, merging into a
golden colour on the sides of the fish that fades into

white or yellowish-white on the belly. There is a dark horizontal stripe running from the snout through the eye and on to the tail fin. This dark stripe has a golden line above it which changes to a copper colour near the tail. The caudal fin is suffused with red, the colouring being brighter in the upper half of the fin.

The fish is a prolific breeder, and it is necessary to remove the parents as soon as spawning is finished. *Myriophyllum* is an excellent plant for the breeding tank. Eggs will hatch in 48 hours at a temperature of 26°C. The fry are easily reared on infusoria, followed by freshly hatched brine shrimps.

Orange Chromide

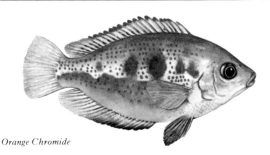

Orange Chromide

Etroplus maculatus   CICHLIDAE
Other name: Orange cichlid
Original distribution: India, Sri Lanka

The orange chromide is one of the more peaceful members of the family and consequently better able to associate with other fish in a community tank. It is also small for a cichlid, rarely exceeding 7.5 cm.

This can be a temperamental fish and will often refuse to eat some types of dry food, or may refuse all food for a time. Usually rather timid, it likes to be with some of its own kind. A water temperature of 22°C to 24°C is suitable, with a reasonably well planted tank.

The sexes are difficult to distinguish, but the male usually has a little brighter colouring and has rather more red in its eye. It may also be slightly larger than the female.

Fins are well coloured, being yellowish, with the exception of the ventrals which are jet black; the outer edges of the anal are also edged in black. Belly and throat are orange coloured, the sides pale yellow and the back olive; along the lateral line there are three large blue or dark spots. Each scale carries a red dot on its base. A pale blue crescent may be present and is immediately beneath the eye.

A second species, *Etroplus suratensis*, is sometimes imported, but grows to a much larger size than the orange chromide. It is greenish in colour with dark bars and may be known as the striped or green cichlid, or chromide.

It is not a particularly easy species from which to breed. The temperature of the breeding tank can be raised a couple of degrees, and segregation and conditioning will be helpful. A flower-pot may be placed on its side in the tank, for the fish will often spawn in this. Fairly dense planting is recommended.

The eggs are dark in colour and are suspended from the leaves of the plants or from the inside top edge of the flower-pot by means of individual threads. The adults are normally left in the breeding tank for 14 days after spawning, though the eggs will hatch in less than a week. The fry will develop quite steadily if kept on a suitable diet.

Oscar

Oscar

Astronotus ocellatus   CICHLIDAE
Other names: Marble cichlid, Velvet cichlid
Original distribution: Tropical South America

This species is considered to be the least characteristic of the cichlids and it shows marked colour variations at different stages of its life. In the wild it may grow to 35 cm, and while not attaining that size in an aquarium, it still grows quite large and makes a corresponding demand on tank space. Unsuited to community tanks, oscars must be kept in pairs and are definitely a fish for the specialist.

Within its genus *Astronotus ocellatus* is the only species of any importance or interest to the aquarist, but by selective breeding an all-red strain has been developed over the past decade, and this is sold under the name of the red oscar.

The oscar has a rather vicious appearance and its characteristics do not always belie its looks. A compatible pair will form a life-long relationship, but others may often fight bitterly. One problem is that the fish is at its most attractive when it is small, and many an aquarist who has put such a specimen into a community tank has later had to make alternative arrangements to house it.

A hearty eater, the oscar demands plenty of live food, diced raw lean meat, heart, and so on. Normal tropical tank temperatures are satisfactory.

The scales of the oscar can barely be seen and this gives the skin the appearance of being made of suede. The body is elongated and oval in shape. The ocellus on the caudal peduncle is black on a red background, while the head and body carry bright red spots. Eyes are set fairly high in the head and the mouth is large. Sex differentiation is extremely difficult. The basic colouring is greyish-green to dark chocolate, marbled with irregular black lines. During the early stages of life the marbling may be in orange, but as the fish ages the colouring alters. All the fins are opaque.

Oscars have been bred in captivity, but it is difficult to induce them to spawn. If they do so, the eggs should be removed to a separate large tank for incubation. A raising of the temperature of the breeding tank will be helpful. The small eggs are laid in strings on the bottom of the aquarium.

Paradise Fish

Paradise Fish

Macropodus opercularis   BELONTIIDAE
Original distribution: China

The paradise fish has a history as long as that of
tropical fishkeeping in Europe. It is a most attractive-
looking fish, but its disposition and greediness make
it unsuitable for the community tank.

Two other paradise fish are reasonably common
aquarium inmates. *Macropodus chinensis* from Eastern China is called the round-tailed paradise because
of the very obvious difference in the shape of the
caudal fin. Its markings are less clear and less vivid
than in the paradise fish. This species grows to 6 cm.

The brown spike-tailed paradise fish is slightly
larger, growing to 7.5 cm. It is pale brown in colour
with gill-covers and head of olive green. The spiked
tail is distinctive and at the base of this caudal fin
there is a round black spot. The scientific name for
the species is *Macropodus cupanus*.

Well-lighted tanks, with not too much vegetation,
are the preferred homes for these fish. They show a

liking for daphnia and other live food, but will take freeze dried diets; as stated, they are greedy fish and may demand constant feeding. Tolerant of temperature changes, they may justifiably be described as a hardy breed.

The body carries a banding of alternate blue and red. The fins are blue to red, marked with splashes of colour, and the gill-covers carry a bluish-green metallic spot. Adult fish grow to 9 cm. Sex differentiation can be based on the caudal fin, the male having long pointed filaments which are usually emerald green and tipped with pale blue. Female paradise fish are more rounded in the tail and have shorter fin tips.

Although there is usually nothing to choose between the sexes as regards colouring, there is a marked change when the time for spawning draws near. The colouring of the male becomes even stronger and black patches may develop on the belly. On the other hand, the female loses colour and becomes lighter and lighter until finally she becomes a dirty white.

The paradise fish is a bubble-nest builder and breed in the standard manner of that class of fishes. The procedure has been described elsewhere in this book.

Pearl Danio

Brachydanio albolineatus   CYPRINIDAE
Original distribution: Burma, Indonesia

There are many *Brachydanio* species, all of them

Pearl Danio

being excellent aquarium fish. One of these, the zebra, merits separate consideration, but other varieties may be mentioned here.

The leopard danio, *Brachydanio frankei*, comes from India. It is yellow in colour, peppered black or bluish-black. It has not been an aquarium fish in this country as long as some other species, but has proved a firm favourite. The species may grow to 7 cm.

Brachydanio nigrofasciatus is hardy but tiny. It is brown on the back and yellow on the belly, divided by a blue stripe below which are rows of spots. Known as the spotted danio, this is classified as a difficult species from which to spawn.

The pearl danio is an excellent fish for the community tank, being an energetic species that is always on the move in the upper part of the tank. A water temperature range of 23°C to 29°C is acceptable. Completely undemanding as regards diet, the pearl danio will always take small live diets avidly. A large, well-lit tank helps to display the fish at their best.

The body colouring resembles mother-of-pearl, reflecting delicate shades of blue, pink and green under artificial light. Of slender shape, these fish have a small mouth slanted upwards, with hair-like barbels hanging from the upper lip. Sex differences are not prominent, but the female is slightly larger than the male and her body is deeper and more rounded, especially when she is ready to spawn.

For breeding, three males are used to one female. The tank should be long, with a water depth of not more than 13 cm, and it should be fitted with a spawning mat or breeding trap. The latter point is vital as the adults are avid egg-eaters.

The sexes should be segregated for a week prior to spawning, and the brood fish must be conditioned on live foods. The female should be put into the breeding tank 24 hours before her mates. Up to 200 non-adhesive eggs may result from the spawning. Eggs will hatch in a couple of days and the fry become free swimming three days later. The baby fish mature rapidly.

Pearl Gourami

Trichogaster leeri   BELONTIIDAE
Other names: Lace gourami, Mosaic gourami
Original distribution: Malaysia, Thailand

The pearl gourami is very popular and as regards care and breeding it can be taken as representative of the genus, but there are other attractive aquarium species.

Trichogaster pectoralis is called the snakeskin gourami and is greenish-brown to yellow with gold wavy bars. A dark broken line runs along the side. The species associates peaceably with other breeds of its own size. Aquarium fish grow from 12 cm to 14 cm.

The three-spot gourami, *Trichogaster trichopterus*,

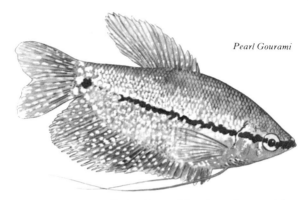

Pearl Gourami

grows to 12.5 cm. It is silvery-blue in colour, with a pale wavy pattern and markedly handsome fins. The body carries two dark spots, one near the caudal peduncle and the other in the centre of the body. The third 'spot' is the rather prominent eye. The species needs a large tank and spawns readily.

Well planted tanks, with additional floating plants, are needed for the species. The pearl gourami needs mature water at a high temperature (24°C to 29°C). It will take nearly any kind of food but prefers live diets.

The body colour is light olive to turquoise with a mosaic of mother-of-pearl dots which runs into the fins. Pelvic fins are long and slender and resemble feelers. A broken dark line runs from the small mouth, through the eye to the caudal peduncle, fading in distinctness as it nears the latter. A size of 10 cm is reached.

This is a bubble-nesting fish, laying a great number of eggs with each spawning, which may be almost continuous during the summer months. When in breeding condition the male develops a brilliant red hue on the belly. It is he who is responsible for the building of a rudimentary bubble-nest. On extremely rare occasions he attacks the female during the courtship rituals.

These gouramis are excellent parents and it is unusual for them to attack either the eggs or the fry. Remove the female after spawning and the male about five days later. The fry will hatch out in 48 hours and are then given the customary feeding routine.

Pencil Fish

Pencil Fish

Nannostomus eques   LEBIASINIDAE
Other names: Knightly pencil fish, Barred pencil
   fish
Original distribution: Guyana, Amazon

The description 'pencil fish' is applied to various species that have elongated, slim bodies, and the dwarf pencil fish, *Nannostomus marginatus*, has been described in a previous entry.

Pencil fish are rather shy and like the company of their own kind, but they will behave well in a community tank. Normally, they are not particularly active, but they can show a high turn of speed when necessary. Soft water is preferred and a reasonably well-planted tank is recommended. The temperature should be in the normal tropical tank range. Pencil fish tend to feed towards the top of the tank, and will accept a mixed diet, though their preference is for live food of small size.

In *N. eques* the colour is a golden-brown with a broad maroon band (bordered above with a band of gold) that runs the full length of the body; it spreads out over the lower part of the caudal fin where the colour changes to a reddish hue. Narrow dark stripes may be found on the back of the fish and below the band on the body is a row of dark coloured spots. The anal fin is brownish and carries a red spot next to the body.

N. auratus is very similar to the foregoing, but the band along the body is black, and this colour extends into the caudal fin.

Both varieties of fish tend to swim with the head upwards, but quickly adopt a more horizontal position when any danger threatens. Adult fish grow to 5 cm and sex differentiation is difficult.

Spawning can be induced only with some difficulty and breeding in the aquarium tank usually meets with little success. A well-planted tank filled with old water is recommended and the temperature should be raised 2°C above that being used in the tank from which the prospective parents are taken. Up to 30 or 40 single eggs will be deposited on the underside of the leaves. They are not eaten by the parents though it is advisable to remove the latter after spawning. The eggs hatch out in 48 hours. The fry are extremely delicate and need to be fed on infusoria for some considerable time before being introduced to more mature food.

Penguin

Penguin

Thayeria obliqua　　　　　　　CHARACIDAE
Other name: Hockey-stick tetra
Original distribution: Amazon basin

Once seen, the reason for the popular name of this fish is readily understood, for when at rest it always hangs tail down, and on account of its colouring it resembles a miniature aquatic penguin.

If kept on its own the penguin is apt to be timid and is likely to remain hidden in the plants, but in a small school it is an excellent choice for the community tank, being peaceful and hardy. An active swimmer and a good jumper, the species must be kept in a covered tank.

The larger the tank the better the penguins will be for they need plenty of swimming space plus some dense thickets of plants. The temperature range of 22°C to 26°C is suitable. Adult fish will grow to a

133

maximum of 10 cm, though 8 cm is more common. By no means a finicky fish, the penguin will eat any aquarium food.

Sex differentiation is difficult. The body colouring is silvery, merging into olive on the back. The forked tail has an extra long lower lobe. A black line, edged with a thin iridescent stripe, runs from just behind the gill-covers, along the centre of the body, and continues to the tip of the lower lobe of the caudal fin.

Although they will breed in a tank, the penguin cannot be described as a prolific breeder. The temperature of the breeding tank should be raised to 29°C, and tall, well-grown plants must be put in the tank. Normal segregation and conditioning of the prospective parents will be helpful.

It is essential that the brood fish be transferred to another tank as soon as spawning is over. The eggs are deposited on the plant leaves but close to the tank bottom. Eggs will hatch out in anything from 36 to 48 hours.

The tiny fry require microscopic live foods once they are free swimming. Many experts consider that green water is an excellent first food.

Pike Cichlid

Crenicichla lepidota   CICHLIDAE
Original distribution: Tropical South America

This long-bodied species can best be described as an extremely efficient predator, and is one that cannot be kept safely in a community tank. There are several

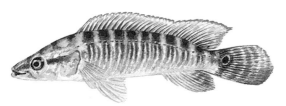

species in the genus though only three or four are ever to be seen in an aquarium tank. This is definitely a fish for the specialist.

A covered tank is advisable for this species jumps well. It is not fussy as regards the kind of water in which it lives, but the temperature needs to be towards the higher end of the tropical fish tank range. The favourite diet of the pike cichlid is live food, but it will accept chopped earthworm, insect larvae and so on. The pike cichlid is a greedy fish and always seems to be in need of food.

Male and female of the species can be distinguished with fair certainty, based on the fins. The anal and dorsal fins of the female have longer rays than those of the male, and these fins are also less pointed. Adult fish may reach a size of between 15 cm and 20 cm.

This fish has a typical pike-shaped body, with sharp head and a large mouth with strong teeth. The colour is greyish-green and along each side there is a black horizontal band; from this band short cross bars reach up towards the back. A black spot, ringed with yellow, is set near the caudal peduncle. The long dorsal fin may be attractively coloured.

The pike cichlid is an extremely difficult fish to breed in captivity. Brood fish need segregation and conditioning, and the breeding tank must be large, unplanted, but with a good layer of aquarium gravel. A few large flat stones should be put in the tank.

It is the female that takes the initiative in the spawning, though it is the male that guards the fry. The female can be removed when the spawning is complete, and the male five to seven days after the fry have become free swimming. The male does not normally attack the fry in the first few days of their life, but may do so if any of the baby fish show too great a degree of independence. The fry mature rapidly.

Pink-tailed Characin

Pink-tailed Characin

Chalceus macrolepidotus   CHARACIDAE
Original distribution: Guyana, South America

This is one of the numerous attractive characins from tropical America; it is sometimes classified in a separate family, the Chalceidae. It is notable for its elongated body, strikingly large and conspicuous scales and the warm wine-red colour of the caudal, ventral and dorsal fins. The flanks are silvery with a metallic sheen that may be green or violet depending upon the angle of the incident light. The back is somewhat darker and the belly silvery-white.

In the wild this species grows to a length of 25 cm, but considerably less in the home aquarium. It does best when kept in soft water at a temperature of 23-27°C. The tank should be at least 70 cm long and planted so that there is ample space for swimming. A small number of floating plants will look decorative and provide a measure of shade. The tank must have a well-fitting lid as the species is a keen jumper.

The Pink-tailed characin is a predatory fish that should be kept as a shoal which will swim mostly near the water surface. It can be kept in a community tank provided the other species are large. Feeding is not difficult as it will take any live food of an appropriate size, such as small fish, water-fleas, worms and insect larvae, as well as chopped lean meat and dried food.

Unfortunately this elegant characin has not yet been bred in the aquarium.

Piranha

Rooseveltiella nattereri   CHARACIDAE
Other names: *Serrasalmus nattereri*, Red piranha,
    Red-bellied piranha
Original distribution: South America

The ferocity of the piranha is well known, and stories of men and beasts being ripped to pieces within a matter of minutes are commonplace. Certainly it is a

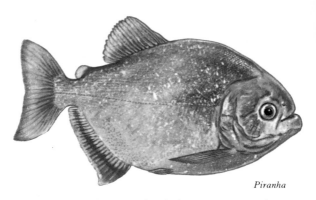

Piranha

very wild fish but one that is by no means unknown
in aquarium tanks, though it is essentially a fish for
the specialist. Even an aquarium specimen can inflict
a nasty bite. It may be noted, however, that the real
ferocity of the piranha is chiefly evident when it forms
part of a shoal, and one or two specimens in a tank
may even appear to be somewhat timid.

Serrasalmus spilopleura, or dark-banded piranha,
can grow to 30 cm in the wild. The white, or spotted
white piranha is silvery-white, peppered with small
grey spots and has the scientific name *Serrasalmus
rhombeus*; this species may grow to 35 cm. The black
piranha, *Serrasalmus niger*, can grow even larger. The
common name gives a good indication of the
coloration of the fish.

Piranha fish are carnivorous, but the practice of
feeding small unwanted fish to them is unnecessary,
for they will accept pieces of raw meat, large
earthworms or raw fish. While a large tank is a
necessity, the fish is undemanding as regards the type

of water; normal tank temperatures suit it well, and the tank need not be heavily planted.

The jaws of the fish are strongly developed, with the teeth wedge-shaped and razor sharp. The head is also strongly developed and the mouth opening extremely big. Anal and caudal fins are more regular in outline than is customary with most aquarium species, and they are of a dark colour. The scales are small. Body colour is slate grey or silvery, with a greyish-green sheen, and the whole body is peppered with numerous dark spots. This particular piranha takes its alternative common names from the distinct pink to deep red belly.

Numerous attempts have been made to breed these fish under aquarium conditions, but little success has been reported. This may be due to the reluctance of the species to spawn in artificial surroundings, but may also be accounted for by insufficient knowledge of the requirements for successful breeding.

Playfair's Panchax

Pachypanchax playfairi　　　CYPRINODONTIDAE
Original distribution: East Africa

A related species, *Pachypanchax homolonotus*, which is less aggressive than Playfair's panchax, is occasionally imported, though it has not been given a popular name. It has green fins with a dark edging, the body colouring being blue or green. It lives in Madagascar.

A peculiarity of Playfair's panchax is that on the front dorsal surface of the body the scales stand out

Playfair's Panchax

like the teeth of a saw. Such a condition is normally indicative of disease, but has no such significance in the case of this species.

Playfair's panchax is not a community fish and is both pugnacious and greedy. It spends much of its time towards the top of the tank and is liable to jump from it. A water temperature of 20°C to 24°C is suitable. Freeze dried food will be accepted, as will live food and all suitable substitutes. It is a long-lived fish.

Males and females can be distinguished by fins and colouring. The anal fin of the female is rounded, and dorsal and anal fins are colourless apart from a dark spot on the dorsal. The colour of the female is also less pronounced and tends to be brownish.

The male (which may grow to 10 cm) has a yellow to yellowish-green body with rows of clearly defined red spots which are also to be found in the caudal, dorsal and anal fins. Brownish or yellowish fins are characteristic of the male, while the caudal and dorsal fins are edged with red and black.

Dense planting of a breeding tank is essential, using both submerged and floating plants. The water temperature should be 24°C and it may be helpful to add the merest pinch of sea salt to the water. Brood fish may be brought to a spawning condition by segregation and increasing the amount of food given at each meal.

Brood fish cannot be trusted with their eggs or fry, and they should be removed immediately after spawning. The eggs are adhesive and relatively large and it may take the best part of a fortnight before they hatch out. The fry (which may be started off on infusoria) grow quickly but spend the early part of their life at the bottom of the tank, hidden in the plants.

Pygmy Sunfish

Pygmy Sunfish

Elassoma evergladei   CENTRARCHIDAE
Original distribution: Florida

The pygmy sunfish is an example of a species that is more popular with aquarists outside its area of natural distribution than it is with local fishkeepers. Another species, *Elassoma zonatum*, is sometimes seen in the aquarium, this being rather larger than the species described below but otherwise very similar.

The species matures very early and the fish are able to reproduce at the age of about four months. The pygmy sunfish is extremely hardy but is made uncomfortable by excessive warmth; a temperature of 22°C is adequate. They are lively fish and for preference should be kept in a small tank confined to their own breed. The males are fond of mock combats in which no real harm is done; these battles give them every opportunity to display their attractive fins.

The fish prefers a tank that is densely planted at one end with fine-leaved species though with plenty of open swimming spaces. When fully grown it measures 3.2 cm. Live food is essential for its welfare, but must be suitable for its size.

The body is rather long and the mouth small and tilted upwards, while the fins are of attractive shape, being rounded or fan-like. At normal times the body colouring is brown with darker spots and poorly defined vertical bars, but during breeding the male changes to a bluish-black speckled with luminous green and gold flecks both on the body and on the fins. Sex differentiation is simple as the female never assumes the dark colour of the male, but is reddish-brown with transparent fins; the larger, more arched dorsal of the male is another sex distinction.

Pygmy sunfish will breed even in a tank containing several of their kind. They are indifferent parents, neither caring for nor molesting the eggs or their young. Courtship is gentle, with displays of fins and much 'dancing', and the eggs are scattered at random among the plants. Fry hatch out within six days and are free swimming a couple of days later. Live food of the very smallest size must be given from the first day of feeding. The fry will mature quickly.

Red-tailed Black Shark

Red-tailed Black Shark

Labeo bicolor   CYPRINIDAE
Original distribution: Thailand

Various *Labeo* species exist and have been introduced
into aquaria from time to time, but these have never
achieved the popularity of the red-tailed shark, have
no popular names, and may grow too large to be
suitable for the ordinary aquarist.

This fish is in no way related to the true sharks.
Many specimens that have been kept in community
tanks have shown themselves to be rather timid fish
that hide away in the plants, but this cannot be
accepted as a genuine characteristic of the species. A
solitary red-tailed shark must never be kept as it will
almost certainly become aggressive. The species is
very territorially minded and once a male has selected
a particular area for his own, he will fight hard to
keep it. Fighting between the males is more spectac-
ular than dangerous and once the victor has asserted
his rights peace will reign.

The red-tailed black shark does not appreciate a tank that is too brightly lit and prefers one in which the water is slightly soft and the temperature between 23°C and 27°C. There should be dense clumps of plants for refuge. It eats all types of food, but seems to like vegetable matter and will browse happily on algae.

The species is recognizable at a glance, having an elongated shark-like body that is a velvety black in colour, the caudal fin being an attractive blood red. Juvenile fish may show white tips to the vertical fins, but these disappear as the fish matures. A body size of 5 cm is average. The fish has two pairs of barbels. Strongly developed lips form a sucking disc and algae, etc., is rasped off by its bristly ridges.

Apart from the very distinctive caudal, the fins are not particularly noteworthy, but have the same body colouring as the fish. It is almost impossible to differentiate between the sexes.

The red-tailed black shark has been bred in captivity, but this has happened only infrequently; much more study must be done before a controlled breeding system can be recommended. The fish is oviparous.

Red-tailed Rainbow

Melanotaenia nigrans   Melanotaeniidae
Original distribution: Eastern Australia

This attractive community fish should be introduced only into a well-established tank as it dislikes new

Red-tailed Rainbow

water. A water temperature of 24°C is the most suitable. It is not fussy as regards food. It is one of the most brilliant and largest of the fish suitable for a community tank, fully grown members sometimes attaining 11 cm. The rainbow is one of the very few aquarium fish to originate from Australia and is a particularly playful fish that enjoys twisting and curving about other members in the tank.

Sexing this fish is not easy, but the male is smaller, more brilliantly coloured and slimmer than the female, while the dorsal and caudal fins are shorter in the female than in the male.

The body colouring is greenish with the scales reflecting blue, green and violet tints; the scales are edged with dark brown. Red and yellow horizontal stripes can be seen along the body. The gill-cover carries a luminous red spot, and the eyes appear relatively large. The two dorsal fins are particularly attractive.

The red-tailed rainbow is regarded as a rather prolific breeder and the fish make good parents; it is therefore unnecessary to remove the adults from the tank. Only a few eggs are laid at any one time and the spawning therefore extends over a long period. The tank must be well planted as the eggs hang from the leaves in threads, either several in a group or as single eggs. It usually takes about a week for the fry to hatch out. Rearing the fry is not difficult but they should be put on a live diet (e.g. micro-worms) as soon as possible, and it will be found that the young fish eat almost continuously.

Rosy Barb

Rosy Barb

Barbus conchonius   CYPRINIDAE
Original distribution: Northern India, Assam, Bengal

The description 'rosy' is something of a misnomer for this colour is only noticeable when the fish is in a breeding condition and it disappears rapidly once the fish has spawned.

The genus has many species, a fair number of which are common aquarium fish.

Barbus nigrofasciatus, the black ruby, is a native of Sri Lanka and has a greenish-yellow body with three or four black vertical bars, but when spawning the male changes to a red colour from mouth to gills, with the rest of the body being black. Also from Sri Lanka is the cherry barb, *Barbus titteya*, which has a dark horizontal stripe along the body with a lighter stripe above, the main body colour being a red-brown. The fins are red in the male and yellowish in the female.

The rosy barb is greenish-brown to a deeper green on the back, fading to a light olive on the flank to silvery on the belly. Near the tail is a black spot that is edged with pale yellow. This species has no barbels. The scales are large and mirror-like, and the dorsal fin dark.

The female cherry barb is fuller in the body and higher backed, the male (which may grow to 8.5 cm) slimmer and more elongated. Sexing is especially simple when the fish are ready to spawn, for the male takes on the characteristic rosy flush which is lacking in the female.

Cherry barbs are prolific breeders but need a fairly large breeding tank which should have dense areas of fine-leaved plants and also open areas that the male will use for driving the female. It may be an advantage to use a breeding trap.

The brood fish should be separated and conditioned on a diet consisting almost entirely of live food, this segregation period lasting five to seven days. The female should be introduced to the breeding tank 24 hours before the male. If a breeding trap has not been installed the plants and fertilized eggs should be removed to a separate tank for incubation.

The fry are not difficult to rear if they are brought to maturity by the usual stages from infusoria to adult food.

Scat

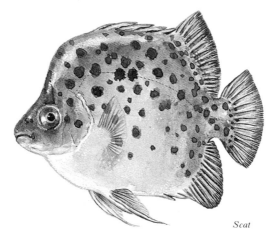

Scat

Scatophagus argus   SCATOPHAGIDAE
Other names: Argus fish, Spotted scat
Original distribution: East Indies

'Scat' is obviously an abbreviation of the generic name
and the fish is sometimes given the longer title.

Although a relatively peaceful and harmless fish,
this is not one for the community tank. It is a natural
scavenger that will eat practically anything and may
be described as slightly greedy. The scat is most
unhappy when kept as a solitary specimen, and it is a
fish that tends to change its marking and colouring
according to its mood and the conditions under which
it lives.

In the wild the species is unusual in that it can live in fresh or salt water and it can grow to 30 cm. Aquarium fish rarely exceed 10 cm. A large tank is necessary with a water temperature of 20°C to 28°C, and although the smaller specimens will thrive in fresh water, larger fish should have a little salt added to the tank. Plants rarely last long in a tank occupied by scats which nibble them down to the roots. Hiding-places of a size suitable for the fish are essential.

There is another species, *Scatophagus tetracanthus*, called the four-spined scat, but this is rarely imported. Similarly, there are sub-species of argus that are of little or no importance, the minor differences apparently being dependent on the region of origin.

It is impossible to differentiate between the sexes of the species. The body is slim and laterally compressed, and when the fins are drawn back the outline is that of an almost perfect disc. The mouth is small and is tilted slightly upwards; the body scales are small. The background colouring of the body can be extremely variable, ranging from grey through green or pink to a brownish-yellow, and it is covered with round spots of varying sizes that are usually dark green to almost black. The colouring can be so varied that occasionally two spotted scats in the same tank might be thought to belong to different species.

Little is known about the breeding habits of the scat and no suggestion can be made as to how this should be bred on controlled lines. This fish is oviparous.

Scissorstail

Scissorstail

Rasbora trilineata   CYPRINIDAE
Other names: Scissorstail rasbora, Three-line ras-
   bora
Original distribution: Malaysia

The species takes its common name from the manner
in which the bifurcated tail moves while the fish is
swimming, resembling the opening and closing of a
pair of scissors.

   Scissorstails are elegant little fishes that are long-
lived, peaceful and hardy. In the community tank
they settle down happily with other species, but they
are basically school fish, loving the company of their
own kind. Aquarium fish rarely exceed 7.5 cm but
grow much larger in the wild.

   Although undemanding as regards the water in
the tank, they do best when it is soft, slightly acid, and
at a temperature range of 18°C to 24°C. The tank
needs to be planted, but there must be plenty of open
swimming space; a long tank with front lighting
displays a school of such fish at their best. They are
not the least bit fussy about their food.

The distinctive bifurcated tail has already been mentioned, and this may be orange coloured with each lobe tipped with a black and white bar. The back of the fish may be greenish or olive-yellow, the belly is whitish and the sides silvery. There is a dark brown stripe along each side which continues to a spot on the caudal peduncle, and goes on to where the caudal fin forks. A second stripe runs from the bottom of the lower lobe of the tail fin to just in front of the anal fin. Sex differentiation is not easy though the female is considerably fuller in the belly.

The scissorstail is not a particularly productive fish and it is customary to mate several males with one female. If possible a long tank should be used and the water should not be too deep. Fine-leaved plants set in gravel must be used to cover the bottom of the aquarium, and many aquarists find that nylon breeding mops are helpful for saving the eggs as these give some protection against the cannibalistic brood fish. Spawning usually takes place in the early morning.

The eggs will incubate in slightly under a week. The fry are difficult to raise. They should be fed on infusoria and when a fortnight old they can be given screened daphnia. The fry grow rapidly.

Siamese Fighting Fish

Siamese Fighting Fish

Betta splendens   BELONTIIDAE
Other name: Betta
Original distribution: Thailand

This is one of the most gorgeous fish to be kept in an
aquarium tank but it is not a community species.
Only one male can be kept in a tank, and in breeding
he is so rough that his activities may result in the
death of the female. Although liable to sulk if the
conditions are not to its liking, this is not a difficult
fish to keep. It thrives best on a diet rich in live food,
but it will take any kind of food, including algae. The
male, which may have a body length of 7.5 cm, lives
for about three years. Normal tropical tank temperatures suit the breed admirably and a tank with plenty
of free-swimming space for display is essential.

Although both sexes are alike in appearance, the
female is rather smaller than the male, is paler in
colour and has less magnificent fins.

Bred in many colours, red and light blue are the
most common. The beautiful fins are the outstanding

features; the fish has a high dorsal and a long flowing anal fin. Such fins may be highly coloured, transparent or translucent. The pelvic fin is pointed and is thrust forth aggressively when the fish is in a fighting mood.

Breeding is best done in a shallow tank, free of gravel but densely planted at one end. The male will build a fairly large bubble nest, force the female under it, and squeeze the eggs from her by wrapping his body round hers and by exerting considerable pressure. This is a vigorous mating and when complete the exhausted female must be allowed to recuperate in a separate tank.

The male catches the eggs and puts them in the nest; the fry will hatch out in about 48 hours. Infusoria should then be given. The new-born fry hang from the nest for a few days and are jealously guarded by the male, who will put them back into the nest when necessary. If given plenty of infusoria the fry will, after some days, swim freely and the nest will begin to break up. When this occurs the male must be removed from the breeding tank.

The depth of water in the tank can be gradually increased as the fry mature and they may be given micro-worm, screened daphnids and other more adult foods. They will be fully grown in about nine months.

Silver Hatchet

Gasteropelecus levis   GASTEROPELECIDAE
Other name: Hatchet fish
Original distribution: South America

Silver Hatchet

The hatchet fishes have very deep bellies, but being exceedingly thin when seen in end view, each one bears some resemblance to a hatchet blade. The bony skeleton of this fish shows a greatly protruded breast region and this provides an anchorage for the unusually large muscles of the pectoral fins. When spread out the pectoral fins somewhat resemble a bird's wings in appearance, and as these fins can be beaten rapidly, the fish can take off from the surface of the water and glide for a considerable distance.

The silver hatchet is perhaps the most popular of the three members of the genus likely to be seen in aquarium tanks. The common hatchet, *Gasteropelecus sternicla*, is yellowish to a light silver-grey and may grow to 7 cm. *Gasteropelecus maculatus* is a larger fish, having a silvery body with cross bands made up of several dots, and is accordingly known as the spotted hatchet. Both species are treated in the same way as the silver hatchet fish described below.

The silver hatchet settles quite happily in a community tank (which must be kept covered) but likes the apparent protection of a shoal, so more than one pair should be kept. A long tank of slightly acid water is suitable, with a reasonable amount of

154

vegetation and a normal tropical fish tank temperature. Adult fish reach a size of 6 cm. Silver hatchets will not feed from near the bottom of the tank and must be given live and vegetable diets only; they will not accept dried foods. It is unfortunate that this attractive fish should have a relatively short life, but this may partly be due to the difficulty in feeding them satisfactorily.

The body is of a shiny silver but is slightly darker along the back. A dark narrow stripe runs the length of the body from the gill-cover to the caudal peduncle, with a second stripe along the base of the anal fin. The fins are colourless. The dorsal fin is set well back and the caudal is usually well forked. Sex differences are so slight as to be indiscernible.

The genus, which is oviparous, does not appear to have been bred successfully in captivity.

Spiny Catfish

Amblydoras hancocki   DORADIDAE
Other name: Hancock's amblydoras
Original distribution: Western Amazon, the
    Guianas

This member of the catfish group is rather unusual in that it makes the grunting noise already mentioned for the croaking gourami and croaking tetra. Some writers have used the term 'talking cat', but this name has not been taken into common use.

A tank with a deep sandy bottom is essential for the well-being of the fish as it loves to bury itself in

Spiny Catfish

the sand until only the front part of the body is showing. It is a nocturnal species and must have some dark hiding-places. The spiny catfish is at home in the warm water of the tropical tank, but it is sufficiently hardy to withstand temporary exposure to low temperatures. Small live foods are the preferred diet, but other kinds of food will be accepted.

This is one of the group of fishes described as an armoured catfish for the body has many bony plates. Obviously it is a fish for the specialist tank and it is capable of growing to 20 cm under optimum conditions.

The body gives the impression of being exceptionally short when seen from above. The armouring of the fish is most noticeable towards the head, while the slightly compressed body tapers off towards the caudal peduncle. Pectoral fins are armed with exceptionally long spines, but the other fins are small; the species has an adipose fin. The three pairs of barbels are prominent.

Its basic colouring is fawn to a deeper shade of brown, mottled with irregular black streaks that may be edged with white. The belly of the fish is whitish, and this belly is peppered with numerous black spots. Sex differentiation is difficult but the female tends to have fewer black belly spots.

A certain amount of information is available regarding the breeding habits of the species, but this is not sufficient to be able to recommend the correct conditions for breeding in an aquarium. The fish is oviparous.

Splashing Tetra

Splashing Tetra

Copeina arnoldi   LEBIASINIDAE
Other names: Spraying characin, Jumping characin
Original distribution: Amazon basin, Brazil

Another species in the family, *Copeina guttata*, is a community fish that is considerably less popular than the splashing tetra. It is greyish-brown in colour with a bluish sheen, the belly being almost white while the upper part of the body is spotted with red dots; these are considerably less numerous in the female of the species. This fish is usually known as the red-spotted copeina.

The splashing tetra must have a cover over its tank. (See the notes on breeding habits.) It is a hardy fish, rarely exceeding 7 cm in size, and it likes a water temperature of between 22°C and 26°C. Food requirements are simple and it will eat almost anything that is given to it.

Although a characin, the fish has no adipose fin. The scales are large, the body slim, and the dorsal fin is set well back. In colour the body is a reddish-brown, highlighted with silver, and the scales are edged with a dark colour. The male grows slightly larger than the female and its dorsal fin has a white spot at the base and a small dark coloured area in front of it. Pelvic and anal fins are suffused with red and this colour may also occur in the lower fork of the caudal fin.

To imitate natural conditions, a sheet of frosted glass is painted green and suspended above the water of the breeding tank. A brood pair should be put into the tank and fed exclusively on live food. When the time for spawning comes the male goes into his ritual courtship dance and then drives the female to the selected area. Both fish will leap out of the water to the spawning area, where they will remain for a few seconds before falling back. To achieve this the fish face each other and partially lock their fins.

The first few leaps will be false matings, then the eggs will be laid on the glass. Up to 100 fertilized eggs will be deposited, the spawning lasting about an hour. The eggs are then tended by the male. He will stay at one end of the tank, well away from the eggs, and every quarter of an hour or so he swims underneath the eggs and splashes them with quick movements of his tail.

It takes about three days for the eggs to hatch. The fry fall into the water and remain at the bottom of the tank for seven days. Once free swimming, a typical regular feeding programme, starting with infusoria, will bring the fry along to maturity.

The splashing tetra is also known as *Copella arnoldi*.

Striped Hatchet Fish

Striped Hatchet Fish

Carnegiella strigata   Gasteropelecidae
Other name: Marbled hatchet fish
Original distribution: Amazon

As with all hatchet fishes, this species has the well-developed pectoral fins that enable it to skim along the surface of the water, together with the thin, hatchet-shaped body. If it is kept in a covered tank that is well lighted, it looks more attractive. Unfortunately, it is not a long-lived fish.

The striped hatchet is quite well behaved in a community tank and grows to an average size of about 4 cm. It is accommodating enough to take dried foods, but to keep the fish in good health it must be given live food at frequent intervals. Members of the genus tend to feed at the surface of the water. Normal tropical tank temperatures suit the fish well, but it likes a tank that is planted densely towards the bottom and has plenty of open swimming space at the surface.

A similar species, differing only in colour, is the black-winged hatchet fish, *Carnegiella marthae*.

The striped hatchet fish is difficult to sex, there being no noticeable differences apart from the fuller body of the female. The colour of the fish is silvery, the back being olive and the sides overlaid with dark marbling, the markings running diagonally forward from below the dorsal fin. It is a slender fish with small ventral fins.

Although breeding of this species has taken place in the aquarium tank, it is still considered to be a rare feat. Plenty of fine-leaved plants are needed in the tank and these must include floating plants. After ritual courtship the adhesive eggs are deposited while the fish are side by side. Only a few eggs are laid at any one time and spawning may continue over a long period. Unfortunately, both brood fish are avid egg-eaters and without using spawning mats, or something similar, it is unlikely that many eggs will survive to incubate. Any fry that survive will have to be given infusoria and switched to tiny live foods as soon as they will accept such a diet. This would be an interesting genus with which to conduct experiments in controlled breeding.

Sucking Catfish

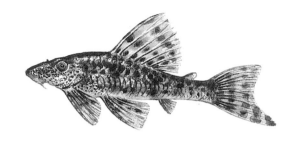

Sucking Catfish

Plecostomus commersoni   LORICARIIDAE
Other name: Suckermouth catfish
Original distribution: Amazon

The sucking catfish is not a particularly attractive-looking fish, but it is an excellent scavenger. Sufficiently peaceful to be kept in a community tank, it can cause some havoc by rooting up the plants. Its common name arises from the fact that it has a huge sucker mouth enabling it to cling tenaciously to any surface on which it may choose to settle.

The preferred tank temperature is 22°C to 25°C, but the water must be clean or the fish will soon show signs of ill health. Although omnivorous, the sucking cat will eat enormous quantities of algae and other vegetable matter. A reasonable size for an aquarium fish is from 10 cm to 15 cm, though the genus can grow much larger in the wild.

Sucking cats need hiding-places in their tank during the day and they will emerge at dusk and dawn to take their food.

Sexual differences are hard to determine. The fish are usually greyish-brown in colour with longitudinal rows of dark brown spots. The dorsal fin is large and crestlike, and is marked with several spots, the back being strongly arched and the snout rounded. The eyes seem particularly small for the size of the fish. A peculiarity of the body shaping is that its front part is wider than it is high.

The genus is a member of the family popularly known as the armoured cats. These have a coating of bony plates covering the body, with the exception of the belly, and normally have fine spines on the plates.

It is believed that the fish has not been bred successfully in captivity except, possibly, by accident. Catfish are oviparous.

Swordtail

Xiphophorus helleri   POECILIIDAE
Other name: Mexican swordtail
Original distribution: Mexico

Few hobby fish achieve the continued popularity that the swordtail has enjoyed. This species, together with the guppy, forms an ideal combination for the beginner's community tank.

The male is easily recognized because the lower part of the caudal fin is developed into a long, sword-like shape. The original swordtail was of a greenish

Swordtail

colour with the sword a metallic green hue, while along the centre of the body was a vivid red line. This particular variety is still seen in large numbers, but colour variations have been introduced by careful breeding. Such varieties as 'double swords', 'sailfins' and 'albinos' are now commonplace.

An unusual feature of the species is that in old age sex reversal may take place, this always being from female to male.

The swordtail is a lively fish and a good jumper, quite undemanding as regards food, though it is particularly fond of algae. A suitable temperature range is 20°C to 25°C. Larger males tend to bully smaller ones. The swordtail is a fish that needs a fairly large tank and it can then display its swimming prowess.

Adult males grow to 8 cm (excluding the length of the sword) and the rather drab female to 12 cm. A swordtail can become mature at the age of about four

163

months, though they should not be encouraged to breed at this age.

Breeding is carried out along the normal lines for all live-bearing species, and a mature female can produce anything between 30 and 60 young every four to six weeks, one fertilization resulting in several broods. Swordtails will produce young in the community tank, although few of the fry are likely to survive unless the tank is really densely planted.

In a breeding tank it is essential to install a trap, for the brood fish have cannibalistic tendencies, though these can be minimized to a great extent by feeding the brood fish exclusively on a live diet. Segregation and conditioning will help to encourage breeding, though it is true to say that the swordtail is sexually precocious and needs little encouragement to breed.

The fry are easy to rear. As soon as they are born they can be given live-bearer tubed food and can soon graduate to finely sieved dry food. They grow quickly and, even if born in a community tank, they will survive if they can escape the hazards of the first seven days.

Texas Cichlid

Cichlasoma cyanoguttatum   CICHLIDAE
Other names: *Herichthys cyanoguttatus*, Rio Grande perch
Original distribution: Upper Mexico, Southern Texas

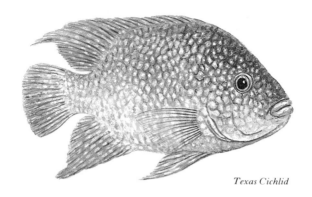

Texas Cichlid

The Texas cichlid is a pugnacious species that needs to be kept in a large specialist tank. It shows no objection to a bare tank which is preferable, as it will uproot any plants it comes across. This particular species cannot tolerate foul water which will soon affect its health, but at the same time it creates a considerable amount of aquarium dirt. Most keepers of the Texas cichlid periodically change one-third of the water in the tank.

The species is tolerant of low water temperatures to a greater extent than most of the cichlids, but equally it will adjust very well to a wide range of temperature. Aquarium fish rarely exceed 15 cm, but wild fish grow much larger. Live food and suitable substitutes are necessary; the fish is not particularly greedy.

Males and females are not easily distinguished, but the male is generally the larger, has a less well-rounded belly, and usually larger anal and dorsal fins.

There appear to be two forms of the fish, the juvenile form being orange to olive-green in colour with very dark bars. In the adult form the colour is bluish-grey liberally speckled with blue or green spots, these extending well into the dorsal fin. All in all it is a most handsome-looking fish. The back is rather high and the eye large; the front of the head slopes back sharply. The fins are not particularly distinguished.

When in a breeding condition the male changes colour dramatically, the upper part of the body being a creamy colour, mottled with brown markings and patterns; the belly of the female gets darker and is almost black in shade.

The Texas cichlid breeds in the customary manner of the cichlids, by laying eggs, but it is not easy to induce it to do so. Conditioning and segregation may help, as will raising the temperature of the breeding tank. This is not a species that is bred regularly, and a recommended method of controlled breeding cannot be given.

Tiger Barb

Barbus tetrazona   CYPRINIDAE
Other name: Sumatran tiger barb
Original distribution: Sumatra

This fish has been the cause of considerable argument between ichthyologists as to its proper scientific status, and this has not been helped by the fact that the description of 'tiger' barb has been applied to so many

Tiger Barb

different fish. The following description is based on what is considered to be the most popular of the tiger barbs.

A fast swimming and colourful little fish, this barb may be annoying to the inhabitants of a community tank by its sheer high spirits, while some specimens are inveterate tail-fin nippers. They prefer to be in small shoals of their own kind. In their own way they serve as useful indicators of tank conditions for when the water becomes foul they swim at an angle, the head being either up or down.

High water temperatures (25°C to 27°C) are preferred and plenty of open swimming space must be allowed. Small food of any kind is taken, but algae and vegetable matter are essential to health.

The tiger barb has a yellowish body with four narrow dark bands running vertically right around the body and head, one passing through the eye and another at the caudal peduncle. The body is slightly arched and, as the fish ages, this arching becomes more pronounced. An adult male grows to 5.5 cm. The sex differences are not great, though the female is less colourful, broader and rounder than the male.

All fins are tipped with red. The more mature the fish, the less pronounced will be its colouring.

Dense planting of the breeding tank is necessary and two males should be mated to one female. Heavy conditioning of the brood fish on live food is desirable. The courtship ritual is likely to be boisterous, and the adhesive eggs will be well scattered about the tank.

The brood fish will eat eggs or fry and they must be transferred to another tank when spawning has finished. The fry will hatch out quickly and will soon be brought to maturity if given suitable diets.

Upside Down Catfish

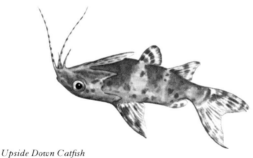

Upside Down Catfish

Synodontis nigriventris MOCHOKIDAE
Original distribution: Congo

This remarkable fish swims and rests in a number of strange positions, though the most usual one is upside down; in this posture it will eat from the underside of the leaves. Because of its mode of life it reverses the normal order of things and has the darker colours on its belly and the lighter on its back.

Synodontis nigriventris is the most common of the upside down catfish, but there are a few other species that may be imported from time to time, usually for large public aquaria, as they grow larger than the species described below.

The fish is sufficiently peaceful to be kept in a community tank, but being a species that is active only in a half-light, these fish can be kept satisfactorily only in a dimly lit tank. Water temperatures of 22°C to 26°C are suitable. Although scavengers, they need additional food which can be varied, but which must contain a high proportion of vegetable matter.

One of the distinctive marks of the genus is the long branched barbels, these often being a source of annoyance to any other fish that may be in the tank. As with most species that prefer to live in a half-light, the eye is large. The belly of the fish is dark and almost black, while the back can be cream to light grey with a mottling of dark brown to black. In the aquarium it is unusual for the species to grow larger than 10 cm. The caudal fin is fairly large and forked with a certain degree of colouring by means of spots and dashes of pale tints. The same tints are present in the dorsal fin.

A species that may be confused with the one described above is the spotted African cat, *Synodontis alberti*, recognizable by the exceptionally long barbels and the peppering of the body and fins with numerous dark circular spots.

This is an exceptionally difficult oviparous fish from which to breed, and although it has been done successfully on rare occasions, there are insufficient facts on which any recommendation as to a suitable technique can be based.

Variatus Platy

Variatus Platy

Xiphophorus variatus   POECILIIDAE
Other names: *Platypoecilus variatus*, Moonfish
Original distribution: Mexico, Guatemala

The platy is an interesting fish and in some ways impossible to describe. There has been so much selective breeding and cross breeding that a dealer is able to stock a red, blue, black, golden, variegated, spotted, tuxedo and wagtail platy, among others, and the name may also be added to moonfish to give white, yellow and speckled varieties. A tank of mixed varieties could convince a layman that they were entirely different species.

It is no wonder that the fish has always been popular with beginners. It is easy to keep, breeds freely (even in a community tank) and because it will cross breed so readily is an excellent subject for quite serious experiments in cross breeding.

There are no problems as regards feeding platys for they will take any form of food. They are particularly hardy fish, living in temperatures between 20°C and 27°C. Platys are adaptable fish and become fully mature when aged eight months.

The female is always a rather drab kind of fish, usually silvery or greenish in colour, and larger than her mate. The colours of the male will depend on its type, the original wild forms of the platy never being seen in the aquarium. Not every platy will breed true.

If breeding is to be practised on anything but the most haphazard lines, it is essential that the sexes are segregated before mating. It will be a big help if a separate tank can be given over for the actual mating and breeding, as it will then be quite unnecessary to move the expectant mother. Gravid females can only be moved well in advance of the expected birth for such movement can result in the death of the mother and her brood.

At her prime a female can give birth to 100 fry over two months and a good percentage of these will survive, for platys very rarely eat the eggs or young. The fry need not be fed on infusoria for very long and they may then be given fine dry food and brine shrimp.

White Cloud Mountain Minnow

White Cloud Mountain Minnow

Tanichthys albonubes CYPRINIDAE
Original distribution: South-east China

An excellent fish for the beginner, the white cloud needs plenty of swimming space to travel around in a small shoal. Accordingly, although they are good community fishes, many aquarists keep them in a long tank confined to their own species.

It is an interesting fact that this fish and the neon tetra were introduced to the fishkeeping world at about the same time. The neon was then an extremely rare fish and its price correspondingly high, but with its successful breeding in captivity, the two species have almost reversed their relative scarcity, though the mountain minnow does not cost as much as the original neons.

The white cloud is a peaceful, hardy community fish. It is easy to feed, preferring to eat little and often. Slightly hard water is preferred for the tank which, as already mentioned, should have plenty of swimming space. Undue heat affects the fish, the most suitable water temperature being 18°C and 20°C.

When the white cloud is young it has an iridescent bluish-green stripe from just behind the eye to the caudal peduncle, but after a few months this starts to fade and is indistinguishable in aged fish. The colour is usually green along the back and silvery with a violet-blue tinge along the sides. Adult fish grow to about 4 cm. The dorsal fin carries a red patch as does the caudal fin, while the dorsal fin is slightly shorter than the anal. The mouth is small and slopes slightly upwards. Sex differentiation is difficult, but the male is slimmer than the female and the latter has the shorter dorsal fin.

The white cloud mountain minnow is an easy species to breed, and separation and conditioning will facilitate the process. A shallow tank (not more than 15 cm deep is advisable) containing dense clumps of fine-leaved plants is the most suitable.

After the usual courtship preliminaries the female scatters her non-adhesive eggs among the plants. White clouds have a good reputation for ignoring the eggs and fry, but it is wiser to remove the brood fish after spawning. The eggs should hatch within three days, and the rearing of the fry then follows along the same lines as for all members of the family.

X-ray Fish

Pristella riddlei   CHARACIDAE
Other name: Pristella
Original distribution: North-eastern South America

This is an excellent community fish that thrives in a temperature of between 24°C and 27°C. It is a fast-swimming species needing plenty of clear water in

X-ray Fish

which to show off. It is both hardy and peaceful, and rarely grows to a size greater than 5 cm. Although the X-ray fish will accept nearly all kinds of food, live foods should predominate. An albino form of the fish is sometimes to be seen in aquarium tanks.

The fish is silvery-grey with a slight brownish tinge, but it appears to be almost transparent. Just behind the gill-covers there is a dark spot, and the dorsal and anal fins show black and white patches, the ventral fins having patches that are of a slightly paler colour. The dorsal fin is tipped with white while the base of this fin is yellowish. The forked caudal fin is streamlined and slightly reddish.

Sexing the fish is simple. The air-bladder can be seen against a strong light. In the male this is pointed and in the female it is round.

Breeding is not easy to encourage. The brood fish must be fully mature (well over a year old) and both should be of approximately the same size. As always, segregation and conditioning may help to ensure a satisfactory spawning.

Fine-leaved plants are needed in the breeding tank. The spawning usually takes place in the early hours of the morning. Brood fish press themselves together and swim to the surface in a motion. At the surface several adhesive eggs are laid and fall on to the plants and sides of the tank. The brood fish must be removed immediately after spawning.

The eggs will normally hatch out within 72 hours, the fry looking like minute splinters of glass. For the first ten days of their life the fry should be fed on tubed foods, and should then be switched to micro-worm and later to brine shrimp. The fish will mature at about one year of age.

Zebra Cichlid

Zebra Cichlid

Cichlasoma nigrofasciatum   CICHLIDAE
Original distribution: Guatemala

This is an aggressive cichlid that comes originally from Lakes Atitlan and Amatitlan in Guatemala. The body is stocky and laterally compressed, the flanks greyish marked with eight or nine dark vertical bars. As in so many other cichlids the dorsal fin of the male is drawn out to a slender point which extends back to a point roughly above the centre of the caudal fin. The gill-cover and caudal peduncle are marked with a large dark blotch.

This boisterous fish should be kept in a spacious tank at least 80 cm long with substrate of gravel and a few large rocks, cemented together, to provide hiding-places. It must be kept in a tank without other species and there should be no plants as it quickly consumes any available vegetation. The composition of the water is not critical, but it should be kept at 20–25°C. The usual live foods, such as small crustaceans, worms, insects and chopped meat, will be taken, as well as some dried food, but it is essential that this species should be given a large amount of plant food. This can consist of lettuce and spinach briefly boiled to soften it and some aquarists feed with porridge oats that have been soaked in water for a few hours.

The Zebra cichlid is one of the cichlids which spawns in the open, usually on the bottom. Before spawning the fish clean an area of rock, a process which efficiently removes any algae. The eggs are laid on this site and then guarded by both parents who vigorously repel any intruders. The newly hatched fry continue to be tended by the parents, usually for a period of 20–28 days. They can be fed on very small live food such as brine shrimp larvae.

Zebra Fish

Zebra Fish

Brachydanio rerio   CYPRINIDAE
Other name: Zebra danio
Original distribution: Eastern India

Few sights are more attractive than a school of these delightful little fish darting and wheeling about an aquarium. More than any other species, they have the ability to move in a shoal as if only one brain were directing the whole movement.

A nicely finned fish which will live from one to three years, the delightful zebra is an excellent community specimen. It is a fast, energetic swimmer and is exceptionally hardy, being tolerant of low temperatures. The zebra will eat all the normal aquarium foods.

The sides of the fish show alternate stripes of royal blue and yellow, running from the snout to the end of the caudal fin. There is little to differentiate between the male and female, though the latter has a deeper body and, when filled with roe, bulging sides. The fully-grown male rarely exceeds 5 cm in length.

Other *Brachydanio* species may be found in the aquarium tank. Perhaps the most popular is the spotted danio, *Brachydanio nigrofasciatus*. This has an olive coloured back, the colour being deeper on the flanks but relieved with a blue stripe. The fins are attractive.

The zebra is easily bred, but three or four males may be used to one female. The breeding tank temperature can be at 26°C and spawning may last for seven days. Some form of breeding trap or spawning mat is essential, for the non-adhesive lightweight eggs are avidly eaten by the parents.

The fish travel up and down the tank at high speed, and after a partial embrace the eggs are scattered. A considerable number of eggs will be laid, sometimes more than 100 a day, but the survival rate is not high.

The eggs will hatch in about 48 hours and the fry will be free swimming two or three days later. The young will thrive on infusoria, followed by brine shrimp, but they must be kept well away from larger fish who will find the fry a tasty titbit.

Bibliography

Axelrod, H. R. *Breeding Aquarium Fishes*. T.F.H. Publications.

Axelrod, H. R. and Vorderwinkler, W., 1957. *Encyclopaedia of Tropical Fish*. Ward Lock.

Cooper, Alan, 1969. *Fishes of the World*. Hamlyn.

Cust, G. and Bird, P., 1970. *Tropical Freshwater Aquaria*. Hamlyn.

Fletcher, A. H., 1968. *Unusual Aquarium Fishes*. Lippincott, U.S.A.

Frank, S., 1971. *Pictorial Encyclopaedia of Fishes*. Hamlyn.

Frey, Hans, 1961. *Illustrated Dictionary of Tropical Fishes*. T.F.H. Publications.

Ghadially, Feroze N., 1969. *Advanced Aquarist*. Pet Library (London).

Hems, J., 1975. *Exotic Egg-laying Fishes*. Buckley Press.

Hervey, G. F. and Hems, J., 1963. *Freshwater Tropical Aquarium Fishes*. Spring Books.

Innes, W. T., 1952. *Exotic Aquarium Fishes*. Bailey Bros. & Swinfen.

Julian, T. W., 1975. *Concise Encyclopaedia of Tropical Fish*. Octopus Books.

McInerny, D. and Gerard, A. G., 1958. *All About Tropical Fish*. Harrap.

Nieuwenhuizen, A. Van Den, 1964. *Tropical Aquarium Fish: Their habits and breeding behaviour*. Constable.

Rataj, K. and Zukal, R., 1971. *Aquarium Fishes and Plants*. Spring Books.

Schiotz, Arne and Dahlstrom, Preben, 1972. *Aquarium Fishes*. Collins.

Sterba, Gunther, 1962. *Freshwater Fishes of the World*. Studio Vista.

Sterba, Gunther, 1967. *Aquarium Care*. Studio Vista.

Vevers, G. and Mills, D., 1982. *The Practical Encyclopaedia of Freshwater Tropical Aquarium Fishes*. Salamander.

Wainwright, Neil, 1970. *Tropical Aquariums*. Warne.

Wickler, Wolfgang, 1966. *Breeding Aquarium Fish*. Studio Vista.

Index

187